A slice of life

CONNECTED BY NATURE

Gerald Smith

A slice of life
CONNECTED BY NATURE

Gerald Smith

First published 2025 by Weston Publishing

Text © Gerald Smith 2025

Gerald has asserted his right to be identified as the author of this work in accordance with the Copyright, Designs and Patents Act 1988.

All rights reserved. No part of this publication may be reproduced in whole or in part, stored in a retrieval system, or transmitted in any form or by any means, electric, mechanical, photocopying, recording or otherwise, without the prior permission of the copyright owner.

ISBN 978-1-0369-6724-6

Text and cover design by Peppis Designworks
Printed and bound in Great Britain by 4edge Ltd, Hockley, Essex

For all my friends and family at
All Saints Weston Green

Foreword

IN THE 1940S, WESTON GREEN WAS A FAR MORE RURAL HAMLET THAN the larger village of today, which now straddles the busy Hampton Court Way that runs between the 'Scilly Isles' roundabout and Hampton Court Palace. Weston Green became divided as houses were demolished, and the River Mole diverted for the road construction that began in 1930. After 1933, when the new road opened, the residents of Weston Green (and their livestock) gradually adapted to navigating the traffic and it was only gradually that the surrounding areas of common grazing land and orchards gave way to housing development.

The community of Weston Green retains much of its own character although it is now more closely connected with neighbouring Thames Ditton. Two ponds feature in the landscape of Weston Green: Milbourne pond to the east and Marney's pond to the west of the Hampton Court Way. Both are referred to here, but it's beside Marney's pond that the church of All Saints* is located. Consecrated in 1939, the 'white church' is a fine landmark and central to this collection of Gerald Smith's memories.

Born in 1943, Gerald grew up on Weston Green with his publican parents and promiscuous terrier, Patch. As World War II drew to a close, he experienced first-hand the importance of home-produced food and as an only child expected to occupy himself, soon developed a love of the outdoors, animal husbandry and nature. With a strict home life, he nonetheless enjoyed a wonderful freedom and became well known amongst local neighbours. From a very early age, Gerald made sure he had plenty of jobs to do, a habit that has not changed.

---

* https://allsaintsweston.com/our-history for more information about the history of the church

School life wasn't easy, but Gerald grew up with the strength of the church community to guide him, undoubtedly an important connection that has remained with him. Leaving school without the opportunity to follow his chosen path as a missionary, he was apprenticed as a gardener at Hampton Court Palace. This turned out to be a perfect move.

Gerald's love for creation is evident in everything he does, from the incredible variety of plants that flourish on his allotments to superb displays in the church at Harvest, Christmas and Easter. He continues to garden, is thoroughly engaged in local life and is cherished by us all.

In compiling this book, I have been in the most fortunate position to indulge my own curiosity for rural life, gardening and nature with a very special person. By spending time with Gerald, in his garden, at his dining room table, reading the stories that were already documented and recording more tales with him, I trust that I have done him justice.

The first part of this book covers Gerald's early life and introduces many of the local characters that taught him so much about 'how life works'. In the second part, we join Gerald learning the art of gardening through a long and fascinating apprenticeship at Hampton Court Palace.

Please enjoy!

Julia Jones

Gerald's early years in and around Weston Green

GERALD'S EARLY YEARS

I GREW UP IN THE CRICKETER'S PUB ON WESTON GREEN, JUST MY parents and me with Patch the dog, and the ducks too, but that's another story. Back in the 1940s, the area was quite different from today and I'd like to describe some of the places and people that made my early years so memorable.

Looking across Weston Green from the railway bridge over Hampton Court Way near the Scilly Isles roundabout, nowadays it's the golf course that you can see. But it wasn't like that when I was a boy. It was a wild grassy area completely covered with giant ant hills and thousands of wildflowers, and in fact, in some months of the year, the whole area would be blue with hair bells, not bluebells. We'd sit amongst a little clump of ant hills (all occupied by ants) and just look at the lizards and the butterflies and as we lay on our backs, looking up, the skylarks would be singing high above us. It was an idyllic time of life.

From there, we could clearly see All Saints Church, a wonderful building which stood out, brilliant white, without any bushes growing around it. A little further along, you could look to the right of the pond to the Red House. Together, the church and house were quite a feature for artists to paint, but unfortunately this is no longer the view as the trees have all grown up around the pond. It was decided some time ago that the pond should have islands in the middle, which were duly created and planted with willows. At the time dear old Jimmy Collins and I stood there and watched them making those islands and he said to me, "I won't be here, Gerald, but one day that will be a complete disaster because you really don't create islands if you've got a clay bottom pond and then puncture it with roots of willow trees." He was right, and that's another story.

A great annual event on Weston Green was Bonfire Night. Every year a bonfire was constructed on the common outside Jubilee Villas, to which I always contributed. Anyone who had anything to burn during the months before November dumped it on the common. This included the Marneys, the woodyard owners who used to clear scenery at Shepperton studios to make kindling, which was part of their business. Any wood that was unsuitable for kindling wood, I would drag across the common and put on the bonfire. Once a week I'd climb up on the bonfire and make it higher, and we reckoned that at Weston Green we had one of the highest bonfires for firework night in the area. I know that Cranleigh still has one and there used to be one at Claygate and West End, but they were nothing like ours at Weston Green. I've had a thing about bonfires all my life, maybe because I'm a Leo, I made sure we always built a big one!

So Bonfire Night was a great occasion. Everybody from everywhere came to Weston Green to enjoy both the fire and the Cricketers, mother's and dad's pub, which was a major part of the attraction. The pub was *the* venue to be at, with music, lovely cooking and hospitality all of which was wonderful. They were well known, my parents, for always helping everybody and it was a night of great celebration.

The Marney family

MANY OF THE VAST NUMBERS OF RESIDENTS WHO HAVE MOVED INTO Weston Green during the last fifty years will not be familiar with the Marney dynasty. As I spent a lot of my wonderful childhood in their company I will include many memories of them, their lives, animals, work and way of life just as I will my literary idol, Mr. Charles Dickens.

Marney's pub, named after the family, is a relatively recent introduction as it was previously called 'The Alma', and always will be as far as I'm concerned! Probably named after a battle in the Boer War in Africa, it had in front of it a straight row of elms of gigantic proportions. Each was at least eight feet in girth and a stunning sight in the autumn. They had been lopped several times in their long lives and had wonderful nooks and hollows in them which made ideal and safe places for the ducks to nest. A lot of people do not know that wild duck nest in trees. When the ducklings hatch out the mother sits at the bottom of the tree and calls them out, whence they topple dozens of feet down, bounce, pull themselves together and follow mum into the pond!

In my early childhood, along the back of the pond ran a massive root system, rather like a mangrove, where the rats lived and preyed on the ducks (which is just how nature works) and in turn the rats were kept down by the numerous cats Mrs Marney had. Neutering wasn't heard of then and the cats weren't fed much either! She used to tell me that it kept them 'mean' and good hunters. However, they always had fresh creamy milk which she got from her two Jersey cows that were kept tethered up on the common. I think nearly everyone in Weston Green had one of Mrs Marney's kittens as vermin control.

The pond was maintained by two of Mrs Marney's sons. In those days the water was crystal clear, full of frogs, newts and sticklebacks; so clear, in fact, that after a hot summer's day playing, I often drank from it. With a gently sloping bank it was easy for Mrs Marney to bring her goats, cows, horse and an old sow down for a drink in the evenings. Not all at once, however, as despite having lovely brown eyes and smiley faces, Jersey cattle are the hardest to handle, especially the bulls. That's where I used to help her.

Her sons coppiced the young trees around the pond every two years, cutting bean and pea sticks. The young shoots had lovely pussy willow buds for Easter and were never allowed to grow and hide our lovely church. It was a joy then to look across the common and see All Saints and its reflection in the water.

Tales from the woodyard

THE MARNEY'S FAMILY BUSINESS WAS WOOD OF ALL SORTS. THEY SUPPLIED the bean and pea sticks from the coppicing and logs from their tree work. Old Jimmy Collins was the chief tree lopper and he would climb to any height with the agility of a twenty-year-old. Then of course there was the kindling wood and sawdust, mountains of it, underneath and around the giant circular saw that was housed in a long, rusty, corrugated lean-to backing on to the pub, which now bears their name. It was my Saturday job to bag up the clean sawdust having sorted out and removed any small pieces of wood and nails. The sawdust was then sold to butchers from miles around to put on their shop floors. I didn't get paid but I could keep any pieces of wood I wanted. I made rabbit hutches, bird boxes, mice cages, chicken houses and the go-karts which we raced down the slopes of the common and hill at the back of Sandown.

> "She sat me down on the draining board and got a well-worn bar of carbolic soap."

The kindling came from the wooden scenery that the family cleared from Shepperton Studios once a month. I used to go with them and ride in their rusty old lorry which was a great day out for me! Once they had to shift part of a pirate galleon ship and you can imagine the fun we had that summer playing in it. We launched it on the pond and pretended the geese were another pirate gang and were attacking us – which actually they were!

The gigantic saw in the woodyard that could be heard for miles around sliced larger pieces of wood into more manageable sizes. It took quite a bit of starting with a handle and the use of many swear words, which, as a young boy, I did not understand. One day, after I'd been at the woodyard bagging my sawdust, I went home and asked my mother what **** meant. She asked me where I'd heard the word, and I could tell she was very angry. I couldn't think of an answer which wasn't going to get someone into trouble, so she sat me down on the draining board and got a well-worn bar of carbolic soap which she stuffed into my mouth to 'wash out those sorts of words'. I never used bad language again!

Old Jimmy

CUTTING BACK ACROSS THE COMMON TO THE COTTAGES AT JUBILEE VILLAS, the one I knew best was where Jimmy Collins lived with his wife and son, young Jimmy. Old Jimmy sort of adopted me, he was wonderful, and a true woodman. He used to keep the common clear and make areas of copse for the bluebells, not like it is now, and he always kept the pond clean, all around. I don't remember really who employed him, because he was a gardener in the Red House and he helped the Marneys in their yard with the wood and he sort of did everything around there. He was so knowledgeable, and I spent most of my young life with him, helping him and talking about wildlife and he used to tell me stories. He was a very wise man, quite tall and always smoked a white clay pipe.

Behind his cottage, his whole back garden was devoted to his poultry which of course, in the war years, was a source of meat. He also had ferrets which really attracted me, and I had a great love for them. Every time I visited him with mum and dad, I had to go out and stroke the ferrets, though I didn't realise what he used them for. I thought they were pets till later in my life. Then, when I was older, I joined them down at the farm. It was a ritual once a month, that Jimmy and his ferrets and all the men that had terrier dogs, (which were more or less all puppies from our promiscuous terrier, Patch) went down to hunt the rats in the big barn. Afterwards they would all go back to the pub and get drunk and mum used to say that it was all good for business!

I remember one year it was a very bleak cold Christmas, and we were invited down to Jimmy Collins's for dinner. Of course, we had it late because mum and dad were running the pub and as we walked over there it was bitterly cold and snowing, but we had a wonderful Christmas dinner. A large bird was served up which we really enjoyed and afterwards, I asked Jimmy, "Can I go out and see the ferrets and say hello to them as it's Christmas?" When we got out into his back garden, I noticed that the large cockerel wasn't there, and I asked where it was. There was no answer, but when we got to the ferrets, he opened the hutch and peeping out of the straw were the ferrets with blood on their faces. Being a little boy, I was very distressed and thought they were hurt, but then he pulled the straw away, and of course, there was the cockerel's head. And then I was even more upset about that, but he said, "Did you enjoy your Christmas dinner, Gerald?" "Yes, Uncle Jim," I replied, "it was a lovely dinner". "Well, the ferrets are enjoying their Christmas dinner too. And that's the way the world works. I didn't keep the cockerel just to entertain you and anyone else that visited us." Even though it was quite a vicious cockerel and almost as big as me, once robbing me of a crust of bread, I never forgot it.

Around The Greyhound

One of the other pubs that featured in my life was the Greyhound, which was a dismal sort of place. It had a landlord and landlady, but the story goes that he had a mistress and because he wasn't often in the pub, he had a manager called Reuben, a young Jewish man who I spent a lot of my life with. He was ready to take over pubs when the landlord wanted a night off and so he often also ran the Cricketers which meant he had to look after me as well, which was great fun.

Although the Cricketers was the most popular venue on Weston Green, dad would spend some evenings at the Greyhound because he used to play dominoes there and gamble and play cards. It was that sort of a pub, and I was never allowed in, because obviously if you were found with a child in your pub, you'd lose your license. I was always to stay outside with my lemonade and packet of Smith's crisps, with the little blue salt packet inside. In my view, Smith's crisps have never been bettered! Where I sat was next to a little cottage which in those days had a wooden weather boarding on it. That's all been altered now, but then it was full of crickets, and it fascinated me sitting in the dark, watching them because I used to collect insects. I really wanted to get a cricket, but I could never catch one.

Alongside the Greyhound there were one or two other cottages including a little butcher's shop. The building is still there, but it's a private residence now. The butcher never really sold much in the shop: a few eggs, some rabbits that Jimmy obliged him with, and a few small joints of meat, enough that he sort of made a living. Next door, on the corner, was a hairdresser's shop where mother used to have her hair done now and again.

Across the road from there was my home, the Cricketers pub. We had 25 white ducks, which were a great showstopper on Weston Green. Mother kept them out the back, where they laid their eggs in the morning and when she opened the pub, she'd let the ducks out too and they'd all walk single file down to Milbourne Pond for the day. And at night, as the dusk came, she would stand on the pub steps and call them in, single file, and shut them in the yard at the back in the old stable. Because they were so well trained, calling the ducks in was something that people would come to the pub to watch. Every now and then, when any went out of condition, they ended up on somebody's table and she would go down to Guildford Market with Mrs. Marney and buy some more young ducks, which was all part of life as you know.

Next to the Cricketers was a long, narrow sweet shop which was run by two sisters, who would babysit for me on the odd time when mother and dad had a night out, which was quite a thing after the war. Everybody was celebrating then so Reuben would come in and look after the pub, and the sisters would collect me, all ready for bed. They'd take me next door and I'd sit by their fire while they read me some stories and put me to bed. And if I was very good, I could go into the sweet shop the next morning and have seven sweets, which lasted me all the week, before being handed back to my parents at the pub.

School days: sitting on God's knee

THE ADULT EDUCATION CENTRE ON ESHER GREEN WAS ONCE ESHER church school, where my formal education started when I was five. By then, I had learnt from mum and dad that discipline was important and knew that my parents were strict. At school, from the start, I learnt that discipline was also administered by teachers. I did not get on well with lessons and spent many an hour facing the wall in the dunce's corner of various classrooms as I had dyslexia which was not understood in those days.

The first thing each day was always assembly. Hymns were played on an old piano by Mr. Potter who taught music as well as other subjects. I remember watching the tops pop off the milk bottles heating on the pipes on freezing days. You then went to lessons. My mistress was Miss Stocks who drove an old Austin 7 and looked like Ann Widdecombe. She was very fierce, always shouting and striking fear into all of us. We had country dancing three times a week accompanied by an old 'His Master's Voice' gramophone which was always in need of winding up and we took it in turns to do that. A few of us were picked out to do a Maypole dance on the green to open the May Fair and many rehearsals were done. Woe betides anyone who got the ribbons knotted! Miss Stokes used to wheel the gramophone out in the caretaker's coke barrow and then kept it wound up all during the dancing. At the end of the day we were all given lemonade and a cake after taking a bow in front of the mayor.

One day a famous artist who worshipped at Christ church came to the school. He intended to paint a large picture of Christ sitting on a seat on Esher Green surrounded by children of all nationalities and costume. He walked along eyeing us all up and picked out some of my little friends. When he came to me, he stopped and smiled and said to Miss Stokes, "This is the one who will sit on God's knee." When I told my mum she said, "Perhaps one day you really will if you're good."

Well, we all had costumes made and I was dressed as an English child. We were gathered together on Esher Green around a tall bearded young man with me on his knee, to be sketched roughly for this canvas. Some months later we all went for a service in Christ church to see this wonderful picture on display. I often used to go with my mother to look at myself, even though I attended All Saints from the age of five. Until one day I went in to see the picture and it had gone. Years later I made enquiries as to its whereabouts, but nobody seemed to know. I'd so like to see it once again.

After these early years at school, and not passing any exams, I went on to Hinchley Wood Secondary Modern taking my dyslexia with me......and that was a whole new experience for me as you will hear.

Beyond the sweet shop

ON THE OTHER SIDE OF THE SWEET SHOP WAS A VERY DERELICT SORT of house, where Mr. Lawrence lived. He led a solitary hermit-like life, although he was from quite a wealthy family, and owned a lot of land around Weston Green which is all built on now. I remember Mr Lawerence because of the way he used to cut hay. All his land was grass back then, and so he cut hay all summer long with a razor-sharp scythe and sold it to people who had livestock, pushing the hay around the parish in his barrow. He always kept himself to himself so nobody had much to do with him.

Beyond Mr Lawrence's place, there were more cottages with various people living in them and then we come to Milbourne stores. That was a very upmarket grocer's shop, but everybody had to go there with their ration books, as he was the grocer that stocked the rations. He took the books and tore the coupons out. You didn't get much, just a little butter and one egg, but eggs weren't a problem because everybody kept chickens, ducks or geese. But I do remember how the grocer used to cut the butter so precisely. Your bare amount of butter was wrapped up in brown paper and each little parcel was stamped before it left the shop. There was no plastic to get rid of or anything, everybody had brown paper bags and baskets which was a good thing. I had to be very well-mannered when I went in there with mother. You couldn't go mooching about and looking at things!

Next door to the stores was the post office, run by a little man who bred giant Flemish rabbits which he kept in hutches all along the wall of his house. Obviously, they were for the table, but I was at that age when I wasn't aware of that. And one day when I went to stroke them and one wasn't there, I was told that it had gone off to see its relations, but of course it had gone off to the butcher's shop.

Then, it was the ironmonger's, which was a dark, dingy sort of shop owned by a young couple that didn't really know the business and inside, it reeked of creosote and mothballs. I'll always remember that, because on the odd occasions you had to go in there, you smelt awful when you came out. It wasn't a successful shop, and they soon moved away.

On the other side was a garage and then a piece of land that was John Dodge's chicken run. He had no end of different chickens, bantams and turkeys there, and his shop was next door. He was a very large man, always smoking a cigar, and he used to sit on a Windsor back chair outside his shop to watch Weston Green go by and talk to everybody. He didn't really do much fruit business in his shop, but he always had a fire going. Later in life, I used to deliver him firewood and logs from Marney's woodyard in my little barrow.

That was what I used to do, always working. I would deliver sawdust to all the butcher's shops in Ditton and Weston Green to spread on the floor, which was the thing they did in those days. I frequently chopped kindling and firewood wood at Marney's, and I'm glad to say I've still got all my fingers, even though at the age of seven or eight I was using a razor-sharp bill hook. I've always worked, so that was that. According to mother's and father's philosophy, "If you want anything, you've got to earn it." And that's what I did, so I was always doing odd jobs.

I saw three ships coming sailing in

ON WINDY DAYS THERE WAS QUITE A CURRENT ON MILBOURNE POND and it was a favourite venue for young and old to sail model boats. I had a wonderful model of a longship in full sail that was always in pride of place behind the bar, but was only permitted to look at it, not sail it. One day, when I was seven, my parents were going to the cattle market, (then held every Tuesday in Guildford) to buy more chickens. It was a day out for them with Mr. Marney. As it was a windy day, I went with my friends from the Red House to sail their boats on the pond. As Reuben was looking after the pub that day, we persuaded him to get my boat off the shelf for us to 'look at'. There's an old saying that 'your sins will find you out' and mine were found out that day when I disobeyed my parents and sailed my longship on the pond.

Everything was going to plan, and all the boats were sailing well when the wind got stronger and colder and my boat stopped moving, stuck in the middle of the pond on a branch or something. My heart sank and I thought of the punishment for disobedience, not tolerated in my house, that awaited me. We all tried to dislodge it with stones, pieces of wood and even feeding the ducks with bread from Milbourne Stores in the hope that they would move it somehow. In the end, there was nothing for it but for me to strip off to my pants and wade out into those icy-cold waters. Deeper and deeper into the pond I went until by the time I reached my boat the water was up to my neck just showing how deep the pond was in those good old days.

With the boat, I waded back out of the water, shivering with the cold and then called in to John Dodge's greengrocer's shop to dry by his big coal fire with a hot cup of tea. He patted me on the head and said, "That was a brave thing to do, lad," and promised not to tell my mum or dad. I paid him back by chopping his firewood then I went home and Reuben put the boat back where it belonged. I took the precaution of going to bed early before mum and dad got back from Guildford and no one was any the wiser. However, I did learn a lesson that day.

One day sometime later, being in a good mood after a win on the horses, dad suggested a trip to the pond to see if my boat would sail. Knowing full well that it could, I agreed, and he really enjoyed sailing it. We did this on a regular basis after that whenever the wind got up, but he never knew the truth about that boat's maiden voyage!

You may be wondering why it was that the pond was so deep on the day I went in to rescue my boat, and why now it's so small and shallow? Years ago, a decision was made to create some islands in Milbourne Pond and plant willows on them, as had been done in Marney's pond. Unfortunately, and for the same reason as before, it was as Jimmy had foretold. It's not the best thing to do when you've got a clay bottom pond as the willow roots grow down and puncture the clay and let out the water.

In Jimmy's time, it was always more or less crystal clear too, because Marney's geese used to wander over from the other pond once or twice a week, stopping all the traffic on the Hampton Court Way, and clear all the weeds and rubbish out of the water, so it was well maintained naturally. Like on Marney's pond, Jimmy always used to keep the bushes down and make it tidy. He had a thing about keeping Weston Green tidy. It was never overgrown.

Oh yes, I remember it well

IT'S STRANGE RECALLING MEMORIES WHEN YOU GET OLDER, BUT I CAN remember Coronation Day as if it was yesterday.

It was what I would call a 'grumpy day': dull and wet with windy drizzle. I had breakfast with tea using my special Coronation mug, given to all the children at Esher church school, and was told by my mother to dress in my best clothes as we were going to watch the Coronation on a television. Not many people owned one in those days, so I was full of questions. The three of us, mum, dad and me, set off in our 'Sunday best', and I thought that we'd be going to visit Mrs Barnes who was the only person I knew of with a TV.

She was a lady my mother cleaned for and during school holidays I used to help her old gardener who taught me the difference between weeds and flowers and many other things. I started gardening there when I was six and she used to let me watch Children's Hour. I loved those nice simple programmes: 'Andy Pandy', 'The Woodentops', 'Rag, Tag and Bobtail' and 'Bill and Ben, the Flowerpot Men'.

I asked my dad if we were going to see Mrs Barnes to watch the Coronation. "No," was the reply. "We are going to watch it in the Orleans Arms." Well, I thought, that means lemonade and those lovely Smiths Crisps! And as usual, with children forbidden inside a pub, I sat outside, quite content with my drink and crisps, watching the rabbits and a fox opposite on the common. I wasn't at all interested in this Coronation thing and it was nice and quiet with no cars, no people, only me and nature just as I liked it.

However, after a while it started to rain and unusually, I was brought inside the pub and sat on the counter to watch the crowning. It was all a bit boring until a large plate of sausages appeared with fresh rolls and more lemonade. After my second sausage I thought, "This is OK," but then one of my father's drinking mates spotted the local policeman coming towards the pub, so I was quickly yanked off the counter and hidden underneath it, but not before I'd snatched another sausage! Strangely enough, the TV reflected in the mirror behind the bar so I could keep perfectly quiet and watch the Queen.

The policeman enjoyed a celebratory drink with the landlord and went on his way. By now I had cramp and crawled out and sat on the counter again until it was all over. We walked home in the wet and even the rabbits had gone into their burrows. You never see a wet rabbit! For the next few weeks my spare time was spent painting a model Coronation coach and horses. Now I'm afraid it needs renovating and repainting, just like my many gnomes.

Secondary school and rough justice

MOVING FROM THE RELAXED ATMOSPHERE OF SCHOOL IN ESHER TO THE rough and tumble of Hinchley Wood School was quite a big change. On my second day I made friends with Little Benny who, sad to say, had chronic asthma and his legs were in callipers as the result of polio. I took him under my wing, sharing my sandwiches and sweets and coat on cold days in the playground.

The Headmaster, Mr Pritchard, patrolled the corridors with a large heavy book under his arm ready to give anyone caught running a good wallop on the back of the head. He also had a long cane to administer punishment in front of the whole assembly. I soon noticed that all the form masters had their own implements for discipline according to their subject. Woodwork: a piece of dowel rod; Gardening: a bamboo cane; Geography: a blackboard rubber; Religious Instruction: a book of Common Prayer, although I never saw that one used.

Religious Instruction and Field Sports were what I excelled in. I did not really enjoy any other lessons and, as you might guess, came away with no qualifications, which was no good as my ambition was to become a missionary. It was not to be, but life is sorted out from above and my long time at All Saints with all my friends would never have happened.

After a few weeks at school, the bullying began. The bigger boys started on us newcomers with taunts and jibes and physical attacks were very regular. I was a peaceful, caring sort of chap and did not believe in violence so because I would not retaliate or fight back, I was pinpointed. Then they started on Little Benny. He could not join in at games because of his disability, and they made his life a misery. He tried to hide but they demanded sweets and money and even got him to do their homework.

One lovely summer's day we were out on the playing fields practising for Sports Day when the bully gang came out doing their evil deeds. Little Benny was standing at the side watching me with my javelin when one of them ran up to him and kicked his legs from under him and then kicked him again as he lay on the ground. The bully ran off across the field with his arms outstretched in the sun and laughing loudly. It was then that I had had enough. I picked up my javelin and threw it towards him thinking to teach him a lesson and aiming to land it a few feet in front of him. Unfortunately, he decided to stretch out his arm and the javelin went through his skin, pinning him to the ground. I was in real trouble now even though I was a hero to all the other bullied parties as well as their parents. I was given a caning by Mr Pritchard in front of the whole school and expelled and was a bit distressed at what I had done. The then vicar, Revd Paul Gliddon helped me through it all and we discussed the story of David and Goliath. After two weeks I was reinstated and the bullying ceased. My mates told me that the morning assemblies had been dominated by sermons about love conquering evil, and peace came to the school.

Sad to say, Little Benny died from an asthma attack later that week and I went through a period in my faith asking "Why?" But with help from above I got things sorted. After all I could have killed that big bully that day but, as always in my life, 'Head Office' looked after me.

I left Hinchley Wood with no qualifications and did not get to be a missionary. I was instead guided to Hampton Court to pursue a great career dealing with creation and the love of my life, gardening.

Weston Green Road

ST. AGNES HOME WAS A LARGE OLD HOUSE RUN BY NUNS WHO CARED FOR the orphans that had lost their parents in the Blitz. These children used to play in the front garden behind a big iron gate, and I remember that it always had a huge padlock on it. Whenever I passed with Patch, the big Airedale that lived there too would come and say hello. He was a friendly dog and I knew that Patch was very protective and would keep any unfriendly dogs away from me.

Mother used to find out the birthdays of all the St Agnes orphans from the Mother Superior so that she could make them each a special cake. Whenever we arrived with a cake in a big basket for one of the children it really did make their day. The orphans who had lost their parents, their homes and everything had so little, and being looked after by the nuns couldn't have been the same. It was quite strange that many of the orphans turned up in later life at the funerals of my mother and father. I didn't even know who they were till the stories came out about what my parents did for them, making life a bit easier in those troubled times.

> "Mother used to find out the birthdays of all the St Agnes orphans."

If we go on a bit further, we come to St. Helen's. Now, in my day, it was a grand country house with wooden shutters and a Roman-style porch which was in a bad state of repair. It was home to a private boys' school, and I remember that one of our ex-churchwardens was a pupil there. The house had a large garden with outbuildings and kennels and a wall around it with an iron railing. There was a cinder path down the side of it, which is still there and ends up at the library in Thames Ditton. Back then when I used to go past it, there were foxhounds kept in the kennels, and I never knew who they belonged to, but they always used to come up to the rusty iron railings, and I would climb up on my little bike's crossbar and stroke them. It was the thing I sort of did with animals. I used to like to stroke everything.

Opposite St Helen's was a double stable block, home to two identical black horses. These were used at well-to-do funerals when you would take off your hat as the procession passed and draw your curtains as a mark of respect. Between the stables was a tack room which, as I discovered one day, didn't contain horse requirements but was full of deep straw and in it, hidden, two young pigs! I learned from father not to mention this to anyone as quite a few people kept pigs on the quiet during the war – something to do with a Black Market.

At the back of St. Helen's where the estate is now was a vast orchard full of lovely old fruit trees and a mass of wildflowers. Mrs Marney kept her goats there, chained up, to keep the grass down. She had an old cow shed where the Telephone Exchange is now, well hidden in the woods also with young pigs out of sight. Pigs like Mrs Marney's and the ones at St. Helen's were often moved from different hiding places when the inspectors came but the local policeman always knew first and was quite partial to a bit of pork himself, so no-one ever got caught in possession!

Patch, our hero

I WAS A SMALL CHILD IN THE YEARS OF THE WAR AND SPENT MUCH OF MY time tucked up snug in my pram in what was thought to be a safe and quiet place on the flat roof over the porch of the Cricketers pub. My father's terrier, Patch, and I were inseparable right from the start. Father trained dogs as well as being a publican and would not tolerate disobedience, and that went for me as well! So, Patch was taught never to get into my pram until, one day, he disobeyed and saved my life. If it hadn't been for Patch, I wouldn't be here talking to you all now, but it happened when I was about two. And of course, I've learned a lot more about this from mourners at mum's and dad's funerals and the old customers that I never knew in my early life.

There weren't many places on the green at the time to take cover from air raid attacks, so mum and dad reinforced the cellar with large timbers from Marney's woodyard. This meant that all the older people could come and take shelter and mum would always have hot soup and home-baked bread on the go. She was a wonderful cook and would never see anyone hungry even when things were short and on ration. The old piano was down there in the cellar too and she'd play along to keep everyone's minds off what was going on above.

One day there came a sudden warning when a German sniper plane got through undetected and came flying our way shooting at everything in Sandown Park. All the roof tiles were blown off causing a lot of damage to the pub and the nearby cottages. In the rush to safety in the cellar, and in all the confusion, it was too late to get me inside from above the porch.

The sniper crashed on to Hampton Court Way, and the plane burst into flames. Once things settled down a bit everyone emerged from the cellar and one of Marney's sons went and got a ladder. He crawled on to the roof through the rubble, fearing the worst. Hearing my cries was a great relief to all, and when the tiles and bricks were cleared, it was discovered that Patch had broken some ribs and some rules and had jumped into my pram and lain across me thus saving my life! After that, Patch was regarded as a sort of hero dog and was respected by everybody in Weston Green. He could go to the butchers and have almost anything he wanted, and father didn't discipline him that day.

We couldn't have guessed that Patch was soon to come to a sad end, but that's another story.

The stables

AT THE STABLES (WHERE THE PAIR OF BLACK HORSES WAS KEPT) LIVED JACK Hawks, a very undesirable sort of man. He wasn't well liked in Weston Green, and this turned out to be for good reason.

Our dog Patch was very fond of this man's sheepdog. Now father and Jack didn't see eye to eye, and they always used to have rows about Patch's promiscuity. Anyway, one night, Mrs Marney was out walking in the woods as was her habit. She could be quite a frightening character to meet, you know, if you didn't recognise her, and she was coming home late from her cows when she heard a shot. She carried on walking towards the Old Harrow pub, where there's now the huge crater, and this Jack Hawks was there burying Patch on the common.

Of course, Mrs. Marney let this all out next morning and everybody disowned Jack. They wouldn't serve him, they wouldn't feed him, they wouldn't speak to him. They made his life such a misery that he left Weston Green, and nobody knew what happened to him. He would have been the proper Bill Sykes if Dickens had been living. He was that sort of man. But that is where Patch is. He's still on the common, you know, everybody went and had a look at where he buried him, but dad wouldn't have him exhumed or anything. He said, "No, he always roamed about free, he never had a collar on, everyone knew him." So that was the end of Patch.

Mrs Marney

MRS MARNEY WAS ALWAYS THE HEAD OF THE MARNEY FAMILY. KNOWN AS 'old' Mrs Marney, although no one knew her age, she looked the same all the years I knew her. She was always dressed in an old mac with a string for a belt, a scarf round her head and her immortal Wellington boots which were even worn to church for rare attendances at weddings and funerals.

She was out early every day of the year, in all weathers, on a somewhat rusty and rickety old bike with various pieces of rope and chain draped over the handlebars together with one or two white enamel buckets. These had large rusty areas on the sides where her cows had kicked them (and sometimes her) during milking. She kept the cows in a ramshackle old shed made of odd doors and rusty corrugated iron, near to where the Telephone Exchange is now. She'd come home in the evening with the cows and the milk, which in the summer attracted all sorts of creepy-crawlies that drowned in the buckets on her way back. She would scoop them out with an old flour sieve onto the floor where any chicken that happened to be strolling through her cottage at the time would devour them. There was, at times, as much livestock in the cottage as there was in the yard!

These were Jersey cows. Angelic to look at and gave wonderful creamy milk, but as a breed, aggressive by nature and they could be quite stubborn especially when being led across Hampton Court Way. They spent the winter in the shed as you do with this breed, but as she had grazing rights going way back since time began, in the summer they were brought up to the yard and chained to iron stakes that I used to hammer in for her as she got older and weaker. These were moved daily as they ate the grass. She had fields by the Exchange to grow hay for winter feed, and she cut it all by hand with an old scythe so sharp a man could shave with it. She taught me a lot about sharpening tools.

In later years she found it hard to lead cantankerous cows and push a bike, so I used to rush from school and take my bike and hers, the chains and hammer and stakes whilst she wrestled with the cows. She was a great loss to me and it's sad when I look at the fields where her hay was. It has now reverted to woods again – after all that hard work in such a peaceful and carefree world as it was then.

Longmead Road

CROSSING BACK OVER THE ROAD, WE ARE GOING DOWN TOWARDS THE Longmead Road estate. In Mrs. Marney's time, it was a vast orchard of old fruit trees with every sort of wildflower. She also had an allotment down there and I would help her with that later on in the years. No lorries or anything could get down to her cow shed to shift the manure, it was mountains high. In fact, her bit of the woods was probably a few degrees warmer than any other bit of the wood. With the internal combustion in the winter, you could see the steam coming off the muck heap. So I would dig the plot for her and stay down there all day talking and looking at the animals and everything. She always kept a sow and a boar for breeding, but I didn't get on with the boar. He was quite aggressive, you know, but he liked fruit. One of my jobs was to collect up all the windfall fruit. Everybody had fruit in those days, and I used to gather bags of it on the way home from school and I could cut through the woods and pop in and see her and help her out. I used to get the apples to give to the bull at the big farm and also to the donkey in the churchyard. So, I fed them all really on the way home and then took a load home for her geese that were in the woodyard, and I'd have two huge bags of fruit on the bike when it was in season. So that was quite a thing.

Well, then the council houses were built, and she lost that land. But I don't really think it was hers at all, she had some sort of squatters' rights. You know, the Marneys were like that, but they needn't have been because they were quite a wealthy family with property all over Weston Green which they let out to people.

Farms, fields, flowers and rats

SO NEXT WE COME TO THE WHERE ESHER COLLEGE IS NOW, AND WHERE there was the Elizabethan Seven Year Harvest barn. It was gigantic, so big that you could get two or three 'Repair Shops' inside it today. And in my time, it was full of pigs, and I never found out who owned them, but there were two men that looked after them. Pigs everywhere in there, and of course, everywhere there were rats too. It was here that the men and their dogs and ferrets met monthly to catch the rats, followed by a mass visitation to the Cricketers for my mum's cooking and hospitality!

But this barn didn't always house war time pigs. It's well known that the settlement of Weston Green has its roots in Tudor times, with a longer history before that. The barn is believed to have been named because it was used on a seven year crop rotation. This refers to the idea from the bible of the Sabbath, so that the farmland would be cultivated for six years and rested in the seventh and that by leaving the land fallow for a year, there would be enough surplus produced and stored in the barn in the previous six years to feed everyone in the seventh.

Alas, the huge barn was pulled down and burnt and the land was sold and built on. The fields were made into allotments and rugby pitches and a bit more of rural England died forever, and walking down Hampton Court Way these days it is hard to imagine how it used to be. A quiet main road with a steady stream of slowish traffic. Slow enough for a farmer to hold up the vehicles as he drove a herd across from one side to the other. It was all fields up to Hampton Court with nice thick hedges and plenty of places for wildlife to flourish. Where the Round Church (Our Lady's) is now, there was a small field where the huge bull was kept. I visited him regularly on my walks looking at nature and got to stroke him over the gate. One day the farmer was there and, being a very inquisitive small boy, I asked him why the bull had a ring through his nose and why didn't it hurt him when he sneezed? "It's to control him, lad," he replied. "You can do anything with a bull that is ringed," and to demonstrate, with a twist of the ring brought the bull to its knees. This stuck in my mind all my life until one day I did this to another bull in Bushy Park when cattle roamed there, but that's another story.

Weston Green was a wonderful place then with all manner of animals in the fields, chickens everywhere and orchards full of fruit and wildflowers. No wonder I was always out in all weathers – as there was so much to see and do, I was never bored.

Rabbit pie

SO OLD JIMMY COLLINS, HE ALWAYS WORE A HUGE LEATHER JERKIN WITH big pockets and I soon found out that they were for the ferrets. He used to put them in his pockets and go out on the golf course rabbiting. He'd ask dad if I could go out with him and help him, because by then he was getting more elderly and he needed to supply all the local butcher's shops with rabbits, as they were part of our staple diet in those days. Mother was noted for her tasty rabbit pie with short crust pastry, and wonderful Cornish pasties. And because things were very short in those days, you know, they were luxuries. One way and another, we didn't really miss out on our meat!

So as we progress back down the road, we end up in the church. Now, I've been going to All Saints for around 75 years, all my life really, and I've probably done everything in the church except play the organ. I've always stood in for the choir and much else: readings, lessons, delivering things, the garden, you name it, I've done it.

Turn the other cheek, not likely!

I REMEMBER THE CHURCH BEING WHERE IT IS NOW ALL MY LIFE, AS IT WAS built just seven years before I was born. The piece of land where the Vicarage is now was allotments, and where the Vicarage garage is now was a gigantic poplar tree, taller than the church, which in late summer shed masses of cotton-like seeds covering everything in fluffy white stuff.

I started Sunday School when I was five and was taught by Phoebe Shepherd, as she was then (later Phoebe Berchem) and Lillian Joynes. I never missed a Sunday and have a Bible for regular attendance to prove it. After some years I became the 'child churchwarden' where, in those days, you had to go up to the altar, collect the offertory plate, stand on the bottom step where the collection was placed on it and then go back up to the altar holding the plate very high and with outstretched arms. You waited whilst the thanksgiving was sung and then passed it over to Revd Paul Gliddon, the vicar. The other children in the Sunday School would try and make you laugh during this procedure, and it was hard not to make the coinage rattle in the process too.

We had two brothers join the Sunday School who were out to make trouble from the start and bullied the meeker members. I always carried a bag of aniseed balls in my pocket and one snowy Sunday one of them slipped a snowball into my pocket without me knowing. I left a trail of red dye all the way up to the altar and had to stand there with it trickling down my leg and onto the step!

The bullies loved to stand on my surplice and try to tear it so my mother would have to mend it when she did the washing for the church. One Sunday we had a service around the pond, giving thanks for creation. I followed Paul Gliddon, carrying the cross, and they started treading on my surplice, letting go just as it was about to tear which made me very tense. All of a sudden, I heard a large tear and that was it! I got my cross and smacked one of them on the head and pushed him into the pond, then turned and pushed the other into the nettles. I had to be suspended for a while, but the mothers of all the other bullied children wrote letters in my favour, and I was reinstated. There must be some truth in the saying 'the meek shall inherit the earth'!

The feathered mafia

MANY OLDER RESIDENTS OF WESTON GREEN WILL REMEMBER THE notorious geese Mrs Marney kept on the pond. They were a sort of feathered mafia, immediately alert to any children coming there to feed the ducks. Surrounding them with military precision, they would continue by grabbing the bread and driving the terrified children away. They often wandered across Hampton Court Way to Milbourne Pond, stopping the traffic. One day I remember they decided to sit in the road. The local policeman came out of 'The Lamb and Star' and tried to move them on with the aid of his truncheon. The gander promptly took hold of his ankle and tore his sock! You certainly didn't mess with Marney's geese.

My best memory of them was at All Saints at the funeral of one of Mrs Marney's sons. Revd Paul Gliddon was presiding and mother and I, as fairly close friends, were attending. Mrs Marney never really dressed up. She wore the same summer dress when it was warm, a heavy old coat done up with string in the winter and always dirty black Wellington boots no matter where or what the weather. On this occasion my mother had lent her a black sequinned dress and had also offered her a small black moleskin hat, all the fashion then, but she had refused saying she had one adorned with ostrich plumes which she had found on the Guy Fawkes bonfire on the common.

Mrs Marney arrived looking like the Duchess of Devonshire but still complete with wellies! As the service was ending, Paul Gliddon walked out leading the coffin. As the church doors were opened for the departing procession there were all the geese sitting on the steps hissing most angrily at being disturbed. Mrs Marney often swore, even in God's house. "Those bloody geese, spoiling our funeral," she raged, grabbing one gander by the neck and flinging it out into the car park and pursuing the others, kicking out at them in her black Wellingtons.

You always gave the geese a very wide berth just to be on the safe side. One day I was riding my first small two-wheeled bicycle which was second-hand and had no brakes. You just stuck your foot in the wheel to stop it. I was coming round the pond down a slope keeping an eye on the geese when the gander hissed at me and stretched his neck out. As I couldn't stop, I ran over him and crashed into the bank grazing my knees. Dazed, I looked up and saw that I was surrounded by geese and was being pecked all over. I managed to flee with my bike and rushed home to mum and told her what had happened. I got a good smack, was told to get my brake mended and had all my wounds smothered in iodine, which stung. It was her cure for everything, as it is still with me today.

Farms, fields, flowers and rats

SO NEXT WE COME TO THE WHERE ESHER COLLEGE IS NOW, AND WHERE there was the Elizabethan Seven Year Harvest barn. It was gigantic, so big that you could get two or three 'Repair Shops' inside it today. And in my time, it was full of pigs, and I never found out who owned them, but there were two men that looked after them. Pigs everywhere in there, and of course, everywhere there were rats too. It was here that the men and their dogs and ferrets met monthly to catch the rats, followed by a mass visitation to the Cricketers for my mum's cooking and hospitality!

But this barn didn't always house war time pigs. It's well known that the settlement of Weston Green has its roots in Tudor times, with a longer history before that. The barn is believed to have been named because it was used on a seven year crop rotation. This refers to the idea from the bible of the Sabbath, so that the farmland would be cultivated for six years and rested in the seventh and that by leaving the land fallow for a year, there would be enough surplus produced and stored in the barn in the previous six years to feed everyone in the seventh.

Alas, the huge barn was pulled down and burnt and the land was sold and built on. The fields were made into allotments and rugby pitches and a bit more of rural England died forever, and walking down Hampton Court Way these days it is hard to imagine how it used to be. A quiet main road with a steady stream of slowish traffic. Slow enough for a farmer to hold up the vehicles as he drove a herd across from one side to the other. It was all fields up to Hampton Court with nice thick hedges and plenty of places for wildlife to flourish. Where the Round Church (Our Lady's) is now, there was a small field where the huge bull was kept. I visited him regularly on my walks looking at nature and got to stroke him over the gate. One day the farmer was there and, being a very inquisitive small boy, I asked him why the bull had a ring through his nose and why didn't it hurt him when he sneezed? "It's to control him, lad," he replied. "You can do anything with a bull that is ringed," and to demonstrate, with a twist of the ring brought the bull to its knees. This stuck in my mind all my life until one day I did this to another bull in Bushy Park when cattle roamed there, but that's another story.

Weston Green was a wonderful place then with all manner of animals in the fields, chickens everywhere and orchards full of fruit and wildflowers. No wonder I was always out in all weathers – as there was so much to see and do, I was never bored.

Rabbit pie

SO OLD JIMMY COLLINS, HE ALWAYS WORE A HUGE LEATHER JERKIN WITH big pockets and I soon found out that they were for the ferrets. He used to put them in his pockets and go out on the golf course rabbiting. He'd ask dad if I could go out with him and help him, because by then he was getting more elderly and he needed to supply all the local butcher's shops with rabbits, as they were part of our staple diet in those days. Mother was noted for her tasty rabbit pie with short crust pastry, and wonderful Cornish pasties. And because things were very short in those days, you know, they were luxuries. One way and another, we didn't really miss out on our meat!

So as we progress back down the road, we end up in the church. Now, I've been going to All Saints for around 75 years, all my life really, and I've probably done everything in the church except play the organ. I've always stood in for the choir and much else: readings, lessons, delivering things, the garden, you name it, I've done it.

Turn the other cheek, not likely!

I REMEMBER THE CHURCH BEING WHERE IT IS NOW ALL MY LIFE, AS IT WAS built just seven years before I was born. The piece of land where the Vicarage is now was allotments, and where the Vicarage garage is now was a gigantic poplar tree, taller than the church, which in late summer shed masses of cotton-like seeds covering everything in fluffy white stuff.

I started Sunday School when I was five and was taught by Phoebe Shepherd, as she was then (later Phoebe Berchem) and Lillian Joynes. I never missed a Sunday and have a Bible for regular attendance to prove it. After some years I became the 'child churchwarden' where, in those days, you had to go up to the altar, collect the offertory plate, stand on the bottom step where the collection was placed on it and then go back up to the altar holding the plate very high and with outstretched arms. You waited whilst the thanksgiving was sung and then passed it over to Revd Paul Gliddon, the vicar. The other children in the Sunday School would try and make you laugh during this procedure, and it was hard not to make the coinage rattle in the process too.

We had two brothers join the Sunday School who were out to make trouble from the start and bullied the meeker members. I always carried a bag of aniseed balls in my pocket and one snowy Sunday one of them slipped a snowball into my pocket without me knowing. I left a trail of red dye all the way up to the altar and had to stand there with it trickling down my leg and onto the step!

The bullies loved to stand on my surplice and try to tear it so my mother would have to mend it when she did the washing for the church. One Sunday we had a service around the pond, giving thanks for creation. I followed Paul Gliddon, carrying the cross, and they started treading on my surplice, letting go just as it was about to tear which made me very tense. All of a sudden, I heard a large tear and that was it! I got my cross and smacked one of them on the head and pushed him into the pond, then turned and pushed the other into the nettles. I had to be suspended for a while, but the mothers of all the other bullied children wrote letters in my favour, and I was reinstated. There must be some truth in the saying 'the meek shall inherit the earth'!

The feathered mafia

MANY OLDER RESIDENTS OF WESTON GREEN WILL REMEMBER THE notorious geese Mrs Marney kept on the pond. They were a sort of feathered mafia, immediately alert to any children coming there to feed the ducks. Surrounding them with military precision, they would continue by grabbing the bread and driving the terrified children away. They often wandered across Hampton Court Way to Milbourne Pond, stopping the traffic. One day I remember they decided to sit in the road. The local policeman came out of 'The Lamb and Star' and tried to move them on with the aid of his truncheon. The gander promptly took hold of his ankle and tore his sock! You certainly didn't mess with Marney's geese.

My best memory of them was at All Saints at the funeral of one of Mrs Marney's sons. Revd Paul Gliddon was presiding and mother and I, as fairly close friends, were attending. Mrs Marney never really dressed up. She wore the same summer dress when it was warm, a heavy old coat done up with string in the winter and always dirty black Wellington boots no matter where or what the weather. On this occasion my mother had lent her a black sequinned dress and had also offered her a small black moleskin hat, all the fashion then, but she had refused saying she had one adorned with ostrich plumes which she had found on the Guy Fawkes bonfire on the common.

Mrs Marney arrived looking like the Duchess of Devonshire but still complete with wellies! As the service was ending, Paul Gliddon walked out leading the coffin. As the church doors were opened for the departing procession there were all the geese sitting on the steps hissing most angrily at being disturbed. Mrs Marney often swore, even in God's house. "Those bloody geese, spoiling our funeral," she raged, grabbing one gander by the neck and flinging it out into the car park and pursuing the others, kicking out at them in her black Wellingtons.

You always gave the geese a very wide berth just to be on the safe side. One day I was riding my first small two-wheeled bicycle which was second-hand and had no brakes. You just stuck your foot in the wheel to stop it. I was coming round the pond down a slope keeping an eye on the geese when the gander hissed at me and stretched his neck out. As I couldn't stop, I ran over him and crashed into the bank grazing my knees. Dazed, I looked up and saw that I was surrounded by geese and was being pecked all over. I managed to flee with my bike and rushed home to mum and told her what had happened. I got a good smack, was told to get my brake mended and had all my wounds smothered in iodine, which stung. It was her cure for everything, as it is still with me today.

Conkers and an old donkey

ALONGSIDE THE CHURCH, WHERE THE VICARAGE IS NOW WERE THE allotments. They were allocated to people in Oaklands Avenue, and I used to help them out if they wanted it. But at the end, where the church hall is now, was a small field with an old tin stable in the corner and two gigantic conker trees. It was here that Mrs. Marney kept a very old donkey. He was retired and always looked very lonely, so I used to feed him on the way home from school and give him his apples, do the water, give him hay and straw, and pick up the conkers. Now, I used to have a business going with these conkers because I was quite an expert when I was young. Not allowed now, but I used to bake them with vinegar and take them to school and swap them for things. Nobody had conkers as big as the ones I could find! One day I swapped some for a pack of cards and came home feeling rather proud of myself, and said to my mum, "I'm going to be like my dad, I'm going to play cards."

She snatched them out of my hand and told me that playing cards was my father's downfall. "You're not having those," and she threw them straight on the fire. And I've never played cards in my life since, but I learnt my lesson that father's downfall was gambling. But never mind, that's all in the past.

So anyway, one day I went over the shed and the poor old donkey was dead. And, you know, that was the end of that era. But I've always stayed with the church because it's always been there. And over the road, were the Brunts, a very wealthy family that lived in the Red House. They'd been out in India most of their lives and the children were born there, and I met them when they returned to Weston Green, when I was about five. We had a wonderful time together because they too had a very strict upbringing. The governess was very fierce and lived next door. The chauffeur lived in the first cottage past Kent's little grocer's shop, which is now a private residence, and it was his job whenever I was with the Brunt children, to take me home at night. Mrs. Brunt was very well to do and rather distant. Mr. Brunt was even more distant and just grunted at us. I always thought this was because he was the bowler hatted man, working in the city.

The children weren't allowed to do this, that and the other, but they did when we all got together. We had

> "It was her job to bath the children and me if I was grubby and dirty."

lots of fun in the pond and all around the woodyard and on the common and climbing the trees and, well, you know, it was a truly wonderful life. Once I was invited in to have tea with them, that sort of became a habit for the rest of my young life. The old Indian nanny had been brought back with them from India, and she always wore wonderful saris, even in the winter, with her fur coat and her sari underneath. It fascinated me, she was always beautifully dressed, and it was her job to bath the children and me if I was grubby and dirty. And then we had tea and they'd be put to bed, and the chauffeur would have to take me across the Hampton Court Way to the Cricketers, where dad would give him a pint on the quiet out of licensing hours, so he was always happy. And I was safely home, you see, from a wonderful day on the common. And that was how it was in those days.

The Brunts had two gardeners, Jimmy Collins and old Jimmy Parrot, who had a greengrocer's shop in the Alma Road with his wife, Mrs. Parrot. That was three doors down from Wilcocks the butcher on the end. He was a master craftsman with meat and after the war, things got much better with less rabbit on the menu. In the shop, like many other butchers locally, he had a huge elm block. This was around the time when many elm trees were affected by disease and had to be felled, so the Marneys made it part of their business to cut the giant rounds from the elm and sell them, perfect for butchery. Outside the Alma, there remained three enormous and healthy elm trees that the Marneys maintained. Little Jack Marney was like a monkey and would climb right up to the top of these trees to lop them, but we also used to climb up them and jump in the pond. Huge heights, you know, you could have broken your neck or anything, but we never thought about that. We had a rope on one and could swing across the pond and try and get in to the churchyard. Most times we fell in the pond, and came out all muddy and mucky, but it was all fun. Of course, when we got over to the Red House we had to have a bath. They had a wing of the house that was the nursery and the bathroom for the children which was huge enough for all four of us at once. So I spent much of my young life with the Brunt children. Then we all grew up and they went off to boarding school and the family moved, so the house was sold. It was a very happy upstairs, downstairs time, and definitely downstairs if you came from the Cricketers pub.

Mrs Marney's cottage

THE MARNEY FAMILY LIVED ON THE CORNER OPPOSITE THE RED HOUSE IN two cottages that were knocked together, and by all accounts, were built in the 1400s and never demolished. These old cottages were, however, in dire need of renovation. To the front was a very pretty cottage garden which was Mrs Marney's pride and joy. It was well fenced to keep out the goats and hens who might venture in to eat her garden treasures but, if they did, they were soon dispatched into the road, by boot! Luckily the road was not as busy then as it is now. The front and back doors were always open except in the coldest of the winter and most of the livestock took advantage of this to stroll through. At times there were more in the house than in the yard. In the back was the kitchen which consisted of one of those old stone sinks (which fetch a fortune now for growing alpines), one cold water tap, and an old gas oven where the water was boiled for the occasional wash. It was surrounded by a mountain of chopped kindling wood which was quite a fire hazard.

The room behind was where the wood was chopped on an old elm block. This was where I earned my pocket money or pieces of wood to make rabbit hutches, mice cages, dovecotes, etc. I got quite good at chopping sticks and fast too, with practice. Through the back room, again full of wood, you came into the front parlour which had an earth floor with old mats on it. One wall was devoted to a huge open fire which was never out as a lot of cooking on a spit took place there. Once in a while, the ashes were taken away but only when they had crept out towards one of the mats. Often, one of the hens would stroll in and have a dust bath and many a time I've seen piglets, that were being hand reared, snuggled up in the warm ashes. Dogs and cats and often chickens perched on the back of the settee, so you had to be careful where you sat if you were honoured to be invited in for tea. Mother and I often were, being old friends, and Mrs Marney would not take 'no' for an answer. Not many people ever got inside Marney's cottage, because Mrs Marney was a very unusual sort of woman. You didn't cross her, and I shouldn't really say it, but she rather resembled the witch in Snow White in looks, and she could be quite frightening. But she and I clicked and she always said to my mum and dad that I was the grandson that she had never had. So, because I got on well with animals and everything, Mrs Marney and I were always friends, and I did spend quite a lot of time in her house.

Mrs Marney always maintained that she had grazing rights on the common and was possibly the last person that ever did. Apart from a large flock of geese, she also had a young horse, two or three goats and the cow. It was quite a challenge getting all the animals across the Hampton Court Way with the traffic. Although there wasn't much, if her geese decided to sit down for a rest in the road, there was nothing you could do to move them. Vehicles either had to drive round them or go up on the pavement or sit there and wait.

Billy goats gruff, very gruff

THE LONG SHED WHERE THE SAW WAS KEPT FOR THE MARNEY FAMILY'S wood business was also the night-time roosting place for all the hens, geese, bantams and guinea fowl so it was quite noisy until they all found their right perches each night. There were also numerous cats and kittens in the wood pile which was over twenty feet high.

The goats were always brought in from the common at night and they too were housed in the yard. I used to help Mrs Marney with them in her later years as they seemed to take over. I would collect old fruit from the greengrocers by Milbourne Pond and give them treats if they followed me. This little trick worked well, and I had no trouble except from a very old and mature billy goat with huge horns. Mrs Marney had rescued him from a lovely old Victorian house which was being pulled down to build the Telephone Exchange by the railway arch at Giggs Hill. The old lady who had the house kept the goat to keep the grass down in what had once been a very beautiful garden but was now very overgrown. The goat was going to be put down, but Mrs Marney took him on. He was much too strong for her and me to handle and once he dragged me out on to Hampton Court Way and held up the traffic. I managed to wrap his chain round one of the lamp posts and then ran to get one of Mrs Marney's sons to come and help drag him back to the yard.

One day he was spotted by an army man who thought that with a good wash and discipline (the stricter the better I thought) he might make a wonderful mascot for his regiment. He was sold to the army and a year later they brought him back to show us. He was well behaved and clean and smart in his regimental colours, a change you would never have thought could happen!

The end of an era

I REMEMBER ONE LOVELY SUMMER'S DAY I WAS LEADING ONE OF OLD MRS Marney's cows from St. Helen's, whilst Mrs Marney pushed her bike with the bucket of milk on the handlebars, when we met my mum and dad coming out of Ye Olde Harrow pub opposite. Mrs Marney told my mother that one of her sons had got a bargain and that we were to be sworn to secrecy. The Marney boys used to go up to London to collect pig swill from restaurants and bring it home in big dustbins in their old brown lorry, which was never, ever taxed or insured or anything. And it was a devil to start.

So Mrs Marney invited Mother and me over because she had a real treat. The boys had acquired a Stilton cheese on their rounds in London. We arrived at the cottage and there was this thing on the table, so we sat down in the parlour. Now they had no floor to the cottages, just the original earth that never changed. They had one tap in the back, and that came from a well in the woodyard and they had a huge fire in the parlour which was always on because she kept the baby pigs in boxes in the warm ashes around the front of it. They had to be hand fed, and that was one of my jobs. I could sit there and feed the baby pigs till they got bigger and then they were put out to people that wanted them.

Anyway, the Stilton was on the table and I was cut a slice of cheese. I didn't know anything about this type of cheese, I'd never ever seen one before. When it was on my plate, I looked down and it started moving! I whispered to my mother that there was something in it. "Oh, don't worry about that." Mrs Marney said, "Get it down. You'll love that, it'll do you good." Well, by then, a cock Bantam had jumped up on the table, which was not unusual in there because a lot of the animals were in the house, and he picked out this maggot. And I didn't think much of that. "Oh, don't worry," continued Mrs Marney, "I'll cut you another slice." Well, by then, the Bantam had jumped on the floor and was having a fight with another one by the front door. So while mum and Mrs Marney were looking at that, I managed to slip my new bit of cheese under the table because I knew she normally had about six or seven dogs under there. Thankfully they had it, and when she saw my empty plate, she said, "Oh Gerald's enjoyed that. He must have another bit". I managed to convince her that as it was very filling, I'd like to take it home. So she wrapped it up in a dirty old bit of cloth and I managed to avoid eating any of it at all. And I've never, ever touched Stilton since.

Just for the records, I've never smoked, I've never had Stilton, and I've never played cards in my whole life! So that was Marney's cottage, well almost. Most of the summer, she'd have the front door open and the back door too, where all the sticks were chopped and the animals would walk through the cottage to save walking around the side. You could be sitting in there, and the goats would come through, then all the chickens. They'd be sitting on the furniture, and it was quite a strange set-up, but I never ever got upstairs in the cottage. Nobody ever did that, but I did spend a lot of time there chopping the wood on rainy days. I used to go and cut mountains and mountains of kindling wood because everybody had fires and wood, and there wasn't much coal about. Sometimes, the children from the Red House would be over at the cottage. They were really nice, even though they were so well to do, and they loved being there. Sometimes, when there were huge trees in the yard, we'd peel off the bark to see all the beetles, so different from the things they did in their own garden.

Even though the Marneys lived right by the pub, there was often a bit of a feud going on with the landlord because Mrs Marney insisted on tying her horse up on the pub fence which didn't go down well. She had a little trap that she used to harness to the horse and drive round the parish to see people. And then, of course, the animals were brought in at night to go in the saw shed along the side of the pub. Once a month, they would get the huge saw going and cut all the wood up. It was so loud you could hear the noise right up at Esher station!

So that was the cottage, and in the end, they were evicted. But of course, as they had quite a few houses in Weston Green, they had to move into one of those. In a way, one can't understand that way of living when the family owned so much property in Weston Road and all over the Green. And sadly, when Mrs Marney passed on, the cottage was condemned and demolished, the woodyard went and it was the end of a wonderful era.

Gerald's apprenticeship and life at Hampton Court Palace

IT WAS 1958 AND I WAS JUST FIFTEEN WHEN I STARTED ON MY FIRST DAY AT Hampton Court Palace as an apprentice gardener. I was to report wearing a clean shirt and good strong leather boots and to expect to work from 7am to 5pm each day, with one break for breakfast at 8am.

The foreman, a stern man, and formerly gardener to Queen Mary at Clarence House told me proudly that he had both assisted in putting her into her coffin and had decorated the Palace when Ghandi had visited at the time of Independence.

My first job was at the South Front, a warm magical place: the sunken garden, the knot garden, vine and tropical border. I was taken to the shed, dimly lit and known by all as the Black Hole of Calcutta. The light bulb and windows were a dull rusty brown from the nicotine of the homemade fags and pipes smoked by the old gardeners. Through the smoke, the spades and forks shone and there was a wonderful smell from the tarred string that was used to tie the climbers and shrubs. I was told to hand-weed the higher and lower paths of the sunken garden. It took over a week. You weren't allowed to kneel. Crouching was permitted but a bent back was the expected position.

Quite early on, I was invited to bet on eel racing on the big lawns. I thought they were having me on but sure enough one lovely morning, when the lawns were heavy with dew, it was just right for eels. From under a bridge on the canal that runs into the Long Water a large sack of straw, with a small square opening stitched in the end, was pulled from the water. It was full of squirming eels. Enquiring as to how they got there, I was told that the insides of a deer or sheep were put in the sack and, as the meat rotted down, the eels came to feed and then could not find their way out of the sack. Selected by size, the eels were lined up and released to wriggle across the grass back to the canal. The progress of the eels was keenly followed with packets of Woodbines cigarettes or Shag pipe tobacco for the lucky winners.

Some winters there were terrible smogs. One day we couldn't find our way out of the park because the visibility was so bad. We lit a big fire, made tea and stayed there all night and when we woke in the morning, the sheep and the deer were lying in a big circle around us, enjoying the heat from the fire. The work was hard and the money poor, but we had some great times and a lot of fun. The standards were high and the gardens magnificent. It is wonderful to look back now at the trees I planted all those years ago.

You're having a laugh!

DURING MY FIRST YEAR WORKING IN THE GARDENS OF HAMPTON COURT Palace I was fascinated by twelve large ducks with wattle faces so I asked the old gardener, who I was working under, what they were. He told me they were Muscovy ducks, brought down from St. James' Park to eat the floating duckweed that clogged the canals. He said they laid good eggs in the ground not like the wild ducks who nested in the tops of the old lime trees (long since blown down by the hurricane in the 80s). Ducks at the top of trees? I thought he was having a laugh but one day he showed me a wild mother duck calling her brood to come down from hundreds of feet up in the tree. Sure enough, the little balls of fluff bounced down on to the ground, shook themselves and, unhurt, were introduced my mum to the rigours of life on the water to be preyed upon by crows, herons and the huge pike that lurked under the lily pads. Still, that's nature!

One morning we observed a Muscovy going into a hole in an old tree stump where she had made a lovely nest of down and feathers and started to lay her eggs. Every other day the old gardener would put his arm down the hole and take an egg for his breakfast, so another egg was laid and so on, until one day I watched a large hedgehog, with the same idea about his breakfast, go down the hole and stay with the duck. This I kept to myself just to see the reaction when the egg collecting hand got a handful of prickles! It was very amusing – well I had a good laugh anyway. I can't tell you what the old gardener said for obvious reasons. Unlike TV, you can't bleep out such words when it's in writing!

Arthur's 'Gunga Din'

I ALWAYS BREATHE A SIGH OF RELIEF WHEN THE HARVEST FESTIVAL IS OVER. It's the climax of a year's planning and hard work growing everything to match, the colours of leaves, flowers, grasses, etc. But as I plan for the growing for the next year, I always have all I need. A creature of habit, I have certain days set aside to do certain things.

Autumn sweet peas are always sown on October 13th when there is enough natural heat for good germination. I like them two inches high by November. The 5th of November is not only for making the bonfire but also for putting the tomatoes to bed and for sowing the broad beans which, when the cold weather comes are also two inches high, tall enough to brave the winter.

It's been a wonderful autumn, warm moist soil and dry weather, ideal for shifting plants about, dividing up perennials and putting last year's mistakes right. Yes, even after all these years I still make mistakes. I remember well my second year at Hampton Court. In those days each border on the East Front had an elderly gardener looking after it and there were two (the finest in the country) looking after the longest garden down towards the river. The plants were in groups with height and colour arranged to perfection.

One October morning I was told to go to the middle border to help Mr Lay, a wonderful old man with a snowy white beard, who smoked a clay pipe and was quite Victorian in his ways. I was always fascinated by the Victorian age of gardening, and still am. As we all walked out that morning, one of the gardeners said to me, "So you're going to be Arthur's Gunga Din then? He never uses a hosepipe you know, always a can." Gunga Din, I later found out, was an Indian water carrier.

We started to take up the perennials, a panel of wall at a time. The plot would be trenched, manured and replanted another day. Arthur told me to get out a large log and a meat cleaver from the wheelbarrow. I gave him the clump of perennials, which he pulled apart, put on the block, and chopped half the roots off. I asked him why he had done that. "They have to make new roots or else they will die." He showed me some perennials he'd chopped weeks before and they were a mass of new white roots all ready for take-off in the spring.

The borders were always replaced every winter and mistakes rectified. As Easter came, I had to push out this ancient, rusty-wheeled, rickety, metal water barrel and an old, long-spouted watering can. I had seen pictures of Victorian gardeners with equipment like this but I didn't think I'd become one! I filled it up with water from the canal and to prevent water from splashing out all over the path, and the public, a wooden seed box was placed on top. And that's how I became Arthur's Gunga Din. He would water everything in, even when it was chucking it down, and I still do that now. He told me to always water a plant in to settle the soil. "You give them a drink, boy, not just wash their faces."

Most people are 'face-washers' today. Because I have a lot of land and a vast collection of plants I haven't made a habit of watering. I get the soil right by digging well and composting, working with the weather and watering in by can, even if it's raining. Then it's up to the plant to search for water, and the rest is left for God to sort out, which he always does. He never lets me down and I think His creation is apparent to all of us, not only at Harvest but always, and it is truly wonderful and never to be taken for granted.

In the bleak midwinter

WHENEVER I HEAR THAT CAROL IT ALWAYS BRINGS BACK MEMORIES OF THE regular bleak winters when you woke up and scraped the ice away from the inside of the window to see how much snow had fallen in the night. But then we also always had wonderful summers, and everyone knew what to expect.

Winter came and with it, week upon week of hoar frosts. The gardens and parks looked magical with the sun glistening on the skeletons of the trees. When the soil froze solid the gangs would set off in the mornings with me pushing the wheelbarrow with the tea things and the old pot plus bread and butter for real toast. I would light the fire and heat the water. I've always been an expert at lighting bonfires, I think it must be that as I'm a Leo I'm supposed to be warm and like heat and sun.

> "Winter came and with it, week upon week of hoar frosts."

When the thaw came you went back to doing the big renovation jobs, but some winters went on and on. One year we cleared 90% of the wood in Home Park, all raked up by hand, and it was a wonderful sight to see the deer and sheep gathered round the dying embers of the fires in the morning when everything tingled in the white frost. It was better still when it snowed (apart from not feeling my feet and fingertips) and I enjoyed observing the wildlife in that melancholy silence.

A few years later we had the coldest winter on record, and the country came to a halt. I remember it so well as I was in my fourth year of apprenticeship and was working in the Stud House tree and shrub nursery. It was nicknamed 'Colditz' on account of the way it was run by a very strict old gardener. It was like being in Siberia that year and we had to help the shepherd dig out the sheep and deer after his dogs had located them and then walk home to Esher as driving or, in my case, riding a bike was impossible.

Olga

SITTING HERE ON THE SHORTEST DAY OF THE YEAR, I THOUGHT I'D GO back to my first winter at Hampton Court. I woke up early, as usual, and scraped a small hole in the frost on my bedroom window (central heating wasn't around then) and saw a white world: the first snow had arrived. After having my porridge, I set off for work in the dark on my bike. It was bitterly cold, freezing the chilblains on my ears and biting at my numbed fingers, despite my home-knitted gloves, and I rode along thinking I had chosen the wrong profession. When I got to the tool shed on the South Front, 'Fagin', the old gardener was waiting. He was so like the Dickens character, tall and thin with a long beard and crooked nose which, even in summer, sported a pendulous dewdrop on the end of it. From time to time, the dewdrop was disposed of by a long hard sniff or a violent sneeze after a pinch of snuff; you always made sure you were out of range when the snuff box came out. Together with his assistant Little Ted and me, the new boy, we became known as 'Fagin, Dodger and Oliver.'

Early one crispy morning, and to get the conversation going as we watched the sun rise over the magical sight of Hampton Court Palace covered in snow, I said, "Well, sir, the shortest day has gone, and it will get better now." There was a pause. "There's a saying, boy," replied the old chap slowly, "when the days lengthen, so the cold strengthens."

It's very true. I then enquired what we were going to do that day – were we to go in the warm greenhouses? "No, only the half-hardy do that!" was the reply. "We will tidy the Black Hole." In one corner, I came across a dirty, black, burnt object with a large spout that I thought was a form of ancient watering can. "Shall I throw this old thing out?" I asked. "Certainly not! That's Olga. She might save your life if this winter's bleak." I later learned, from Little Ted, that Olga was presented to the South Front Gang by Lady Olga, the 'Grace and Favour'* widow of a Field Marshal and that the namesake in the shed went back as far as the Boer War in Africa where it had been used to brew tea for the British troops.

Next day the snow was deeper, and all the gangs were sent out into Home Park to clear the avenues of fallen wood and to burn it. Olga was loaded into a wheelbarrow with paper, matches, an axe and a hammer, with which I was told to break up the ice. "Surely we should take water with us." I said. "You'll get that from the Long Water, boy," I was told. So, the three of us set out across the East Front with its biting wind, the old chap leading, me behind with the barrow with the tools and Olga on it, and Little Ted behind. I felt like the pageboy following Good King Wenceslas as I followed in his footsteps.

My first job was to get the fire going, which I've always been a dab hand at, even as a little boy. I then had to take the barrow and hammer and get the ice from the Long Water, which was put into Olga, and she was bedded in the hot ashes on the edge of a huge fire until she boiled and the tea was made. I was very dubious about having a cup and said that the water was dirty. "Well, boy, it's boiled, and no-one has ever died yet from it. Do you want it or are you going to get colder?" So I had a cup. It was hot, dark and sweet and a Godsend on such a bleak day. Later on, toast was prepared using a forked stick cut with a very long handle as the fires were huge and gave out an intense heat. We had to keep going in that cold and to create enough body heat as we progressed up the palace avenues towards Kingston, collecting hot embers in the wheelbarrow, we ran with them, so the barrow would not catch fire, and started the next fire further on.

As I sat by the fire in the snow and gazed out across the park to the herds of deer under those ancient branches of giant cedars, straining under the

---

*   Residents of apartments in Royal Palaces provided for those who had given special service to the Royal Family.

weight of the snow, I couldn't quite take in the peace, silence and stillness of such a perfect winter's day. I decided then that the Lord meant me to be in this profession – being me, being here, and in the midst of creation at all times of the year.

Behind the scenes

AS SOON AS I TAKE DOWN THE PORCH DECORATIONS AFTER CHRISTMAS, I start thinking about the Easter ones, especially for the church garden. After a cold winter and with Easter being late the following year, I knew there would be problems.

As the months passed, I watched the daffs, forsythia and all my material come and go. The hard winter also took its toll and looking at my vast rows of rosemary all dead I had to think about the hedge I always have around the base of the Easter Garden. The variety I grow for that is 'Jessup's Upright' and it must have been around in Tudor times, but under another name, as it was grown up walls to ward off evil spirits and snakes. History tells us that 'it never grew higher than God' so Jesus must have been about six feet tall as I've never got it to grow any higher than that on a south wall!

So, I had to think about what to have instead of the rosemary and whilst having tea in the Hinchley Wood greengrocer's, which I did every day, I thought of the imitation grass they use in the shop. Then I found some imitation garlands which I stitched on using a heavy old darning needle and fuse wire, not cotton as it is heavy material. That took all day on my front lawn and then I had to find green-topped drawing pins (to fix the 'grass' to the Easter Garden surround) but as that proved impossible, I painted some.

There was also the moss problem. It was dry and being a late season, all the nettles had grown too high so I got stung to bits collecting it and then soaked it for a fortnight to get it green. Next came the little trees. Normally, in an early Easter, I'd force them into leaf in the warm but this year I would have to hold them back a month. Everything had to come out of my fridge to put in the trees so that they'd think it was winter until I could bring them out into warm light so that they'd think it was spring. Good job I'm a bachelor and could do all these strange things!

On Holy Saturday, after a 6am start on the outside porch decorations, it took shape using a mixture of real and artificial flowers which I have collected on my travels. It turned out well and our lovely church looked beautiful with a glorious service to commemorate triumph over death and rebirth of the creation of a truly wonderful spring as everything had true rest the previous winter, even me – I stayed in out of the cold for once.

Head over heels

PEOPLE OFTEN ASK ME WHO TAUGHT ME TO DECORATE WITH FLOWERS, BUT I am self-taught having been thrown in at the deep end at Hampton Court. One day, in the second year of my seven-year apprenticeship, I was doing my time in the nursery. It was always the job of the old and, I might say, rather portly, heavy-smoking and -drinking 'propagator' to arrange the flowers for state occasions. My job was to help him gather the flowers and to fetch and carry for him. In those days that green foam flower arranging material was not about and instead, small wire meshed netting was moulded with bare hands into shapes to fit the vases. Gloves were forbidden; you were told to 'be a man and get your hands hard.'

> "I got up and started to resuscitate him until help arrived."

Well, it was one of those occasions when Mrs Thatcher was coming with her friends for a dinner and I had to hump all these buckets of flowers up the Kings' Staircase ready for the old chap to arrange. By about the thirtieth trip I was quite exhausted and it was then that he arrived, puffing on his fag as usual. As I followed behind him carrying a large bunch of white Chrysanths for the table in the Great Hall, he suddenly fell backwards onto me, having had a massive heart attack. I took all the weight, banging my head as we both went down, him on top of me and me on top of the Chrysanths.

I got up and started to resuscitate him until help arrived and the old foreman came to assess the situation. I asked him what was to happen now, thinking he would take over. "Well, boy, I've got a fishing match this afternoon. It's up to you, but I think you can do it. I know you took notice of how to arrange flowers, unlike the other lads so you'll be fine today, and you'll go far in your career." And off he went, and very nervously I did the arrangements and, having plenty of materials, excelled myself. Two days later I was called into the office and was told that Mrs. Thatcher herself had commented on how lovely the flowers had looked.

The old chap made a complete recovery, and I always helped him on state occasions after that!

Water, water everywhere

THROUGHOUT ALL THE YEARS I WAS AT HAMPTON COURT PALACE THERE were a great many events, functions and sumptuous banquets that took place in this wonderful venue with its beautiful gardens and park. One I recall most of all, because we were severely reprimanded through no fault of our own, was when the Royal Coaching Club, of whom Prince Philip was president, was to have a drive around the East Front and Home Park in the wonderfully restored old coaches and carriages drawn by either four or six immaculate horses. Quite a skilful feat, I must say.

We always had a year's notice for such an event, as much would be involved on top of our ordinary work. So, one day, all the organisers arrived from Buckingham Palace to inspect the route to be taken and to inform our boss that the emblem of the Club was the blue cornflower and that the nursery had to provide thousands of them to decorate the Great Hall staircase and the tables at the banquet. I'm glad it wasn't me that had that responsibility, as it came under the greenhouse staff and was a nightmare for them as they experimented with sowing times, planting out, etc. to get them just right for one evening. I shudder to think what it cost.

The evening came and we had got all the gardens and park tidy and hidden ourselves discretely in the rhododendron bushes to watch as the teams of horses were harnessed to their coaches ready for take-off – all thoroughbreds and a bit frisky to manage. Everything went off well and it was quite a spectacle to witness. However, later in the week a complaint came down from head office saying that there was too much dust kicked up over HRH and his coach and that next year the Broad Walk would have to be watered well before the event took place. Because of all the extra work and the trauma of the cornflowers, we had all been hoping that the Club would find another park, but no!

A year later, in mid-June, and it was time for the carriage drive to take place again. Strict orders were given – no dust on the East Front. Each gang had a section to rake and water well, and our gang took the big bend at the end of the Broad Walk overlooking the river as it was always a bit damper there due to an old spring which supplied water to the Tudor Palace. As the water pressure was bad, and it was a situation where the first on the line got the pressure, we decided to connect to a fire hydrant, which was forbidden. We got in to work at the crack of dawn and flooded our section before anyone was about then cleaned and raked it, but it was still a bit soggy. Still, Ted said to me that the sun would be coming out and it would be just right by the evening.

As the morning progressed, the skies got darker and darker, with a most violent thunderstorm and it rained and rained. We all thought the drive would be cancelled but the sun came out and it was a beautiful evening, so we took up our hiding places in the bushes to watch.

All the coaches assembled in front of the Palace for the off. HRH was in the lea, as usual, and they all sped past us with great gusto until they got to the notorious bend, where the wheels sank deeper and deeper into the hoggin.* As the coach ground to a halt, all the rest of the coaches made emergency stops (not easy with horses!) and there was quite a pandemonium. After recovering the horses, the carriages were left covered in muck and had to be pulled out by our old tractor driver. Ted said to me, "I think I'll have a 'sicky' tomorrow. Heads will roll, matey, and they could be ours!"

Well, they did complain, and I argued that it was 'the will of God' making it rain so much and that we had done what we had been told to do to settle the dust. We were suspended for a week as a punishment. As it turned out, I could use the time to work on my own allotment instead, quite a nice way to spend a week I must say!

---

* hoggin: a path made of red clay and small pebbles which dries out and sets like concrete.

That event never took place again at Hampton Court and the nursery staff never grew blue cornflowers all the years I was there. We were never found out for using the fire hoses either!

The beast

ONE DAY IN LATE AUTUMN THE SOUTH FRONT GANG WERE SENT OVER as usual to the to the Royal Paddocks to clean up the gardens of the stud manager and the Queen's racing manager. They lived next door to each other and were both wonderful gentlemen. The racing manager always knew when the royals were coming to the stud, and he would let me know so that everything would be spic and span when they arrived.

We were sitting in his kitchen, having a cup of tea with him and his wife, when the 'phone rang to say that Windsor Castle were bringing 'The Beast' that afternoon. The Racing Manager was not at all happy and alerted the staff to see that the paddock on the Home Park side of the road was ready and safe as he certainly was not having this animal in the Bushy Park side paddock. This area was where the brood mares, carriage horses and polo team ponies were housed so that an eye could always be kept on them. The Home Park side paddocks were also where retired horses were put to end their days and, occasionally, small herds of deer were caught and put in there before being shipped off to other parks to mix the bloodstock.

I asked the Racing Manager what the beast was. Some strange creature from a menagerie perhaps? "No," he replied, "it's a pure white stallion with a very evil disposition." The horse had been given to one of the royals as a present from a prince somewhere and it had already killed another horse in the mews in London and had been sent to Windsor for training. This had proved impossible, and it had seriously injured another horse and put a groom in hospital so now we were to keep it here, in solitude.

As we left work that day, the big gates opened and in came the horsebox. You could hear the contents snorting and kicking the sides, the sounds of a very angry horse indeed. We never imagined that one day we would come face to face with it. The second paddock has a small, locked gate leading into Home Park where some of us and various 'Grace and Favour' residents had allotments. They were small but very nice, running along one side of the paddock wall and all fenced off with their own little gate to keep any animals out. Now the distance from the enclosure gate to the one leading into Home Park was about five hundred yards; five hundred yards to safety as we found out.

One frosty morning the ground was very slippery and the stud manager's wife, Little Ted and I decided to inspect the allotment and, as we walked alongside the fence, the beast appeared from nowhere. Snorting and stamping, he started galloping down the paddock. The only thing to do was to make a dash for it to the gate into the Park, but as we looked back for Little Ted, we saw that he had slipped over and was clutching a large rock. "You go on," he shouted "unlock the gate and I'll hit the horse with this rock and keep him back!"

Well, we would all have ended up in court or the Tower for attacking a Royal horse, so we grabbed Ted and dragged him through the mud and just managed to escape into the Park along with the rock that he was still clutching. Little Ted took off his glasses and we laughed as he looked just like a little panda but in reverse. He was not at all amused, however, as he had lost his dentures somewhere in the paddock. We found them in the mud some days later and they were taken for repair to the old carpenter's shop and stuck together with his own recipe for the glue that he used to repair the carvings in the state rooms. They were the only false teeth that seemed to resemble crazy paving as, like his glasses, they had been mended so many times, broken when he was in goal playing football at lunchtimes in the park.

A few weeks later, early one winter's morning, we heard a shot. We later learned that the beast had been put down after severely injuring the groom that fed him. It was a sad end to a magnificent animal but one with a big problem. I kept the rock as a memento of an unforgettable morning!

A very special award

YET AGAIN, THIS LAST REMEMBRANCE SUNDAY, I WAS ASKED BY SEVERAL people as to the significance of the two small pieces of jewellery, in the form of olive leaves, that I wore on my lapel. Were they from the Holy Land on one of my visits or, perhaps given to me by my late mother and were of sentimental value? "Neither," I replied, "the Queen presented me with them. They are given to a few people as her own personal form of gratitude for bravery." As I'm a modest type of chap, I don't mention it, but I have been told I should one day tell the story.

It all happened way back in early June 1974. It had been decided that a survey was to be undertaken at the Palace that would take several years. In fact, it took ten years. Two of the people doing the survey came around the South Front to measure everything up. They never ventured out in the winter from their warm offices in the barrack block where everything was written down, but in the summer, they enjoyed their tea breaks with us in our shed. On this particular day, their task was to survey the underground maze of Tudor culverts alongside the old vine border down to the river. Upon lifting up the manhole cover, they found a six-foot drop into darkness, with small iron steps in the wall leading to the rotting, smelly slush you get in sewers. So down they went, in all their protective gear not getting dirty like us gardeners. This went on for days, but they always came up punctually for their tea, I must say! As time went on, the further they went down the four-foot-high dark and smelly tunnel, a pump was installed to clear the way.

However, one day they did not come up for their tea. Little Ted was most annoyed as his brew was getting stewed, so I shouted down the hole. There was no reply and I could smell the fumes. I said to Little Ted, "Something's wrong for them to miss tea. I'm going down." Well, I crawled along on all fours. It was dark, smelly and slippery but, thinking back, I was amazed, feeling along the walls in the dark, that there were vine roots taking up nourishment well away from the border outside that was specially kept free for the vine. Further down, I heard the pump, and the air was full of fumes. I found the two men, face down in the mud. There was no time to see if they were dead or alive but only to get them out. There was very little room, but I got hold of the first one. It was difficult to move his deadweight body and slippery to hold so I turned him over, face up, and crawled backwards, dragging him along to the shaft where I somehow managed to get him on my shoulders and climb up the iron steps where Little Ted pulled him out. I was gasping for breath, but I managed to give him the kiss of life and get him breathing. By now, help had arrived and, knowing where the other man lay, I went down again into the dark and managed to turn off the pump. The fumes and smoke were getting to me, but I seemed to have been given super strength that day and God was with me. Yes, another one of my nine lives nearly gone! I dragged the second man out as he was, deadweight and slippery as an eel, before I was overcome with fumes and passed out. I came round in the ambulance on the way to hospital where I was told that there was some lung damage but that I had been very lucky to get away with my life.

I soon went back to work and several weeks later, a large envelope was delivered from the Royal Humane Society Awards people with a certificate inscribed on vellum, 'For Services Rendered.' A week later came a recorded delivery of a small certificate enclosed in red velvet which read:

'By the Queen's order, the name of Matthew Gerald Smith, gardener of Hampton Court Palace, Department of the Environment, was published in the London Gazette on the 18th June, 1974 as commended for brave conduct. I am charged to express Her Majesty's high appreciation of the service rendered.

Harold Wilson
Prime Minister
First Lord of the Treasury.'

Sometime later, at a ceremony, the Queen presented me with my award and congratulated me for 'your prompt action, which was taken with complete disregard for your own safety and the extremely unpleasant conditions, (which) may well have saved the lives of those men.'

Luckily, both surveyors made complete recoveries and we kept in touch for years until they died. I'm still here to tell the tale but, as a mate of mine said as a joke, "The devil takes care of his own," but I know who takes care of me! It seems it was one of those many times in my life that I was in the right place at the right time and I'm never alone.

So, it might not be a medal that I wear on Remembrance Day but two small sprays of olive leaves. They are very special, a small personal thing given to me by a very special person.

Colditz

A WHILE AGO I WATCHED A DOCUMENTARY ON OUR COLDEST WINTER AND how England came to a halt, and it made me think about our last cold winter of '63. It started to snow at Christmas and went on until March with no let up and yet, in those days, the country plodded on regardless, buses and trains continued to run and people walked and got to work through blizzards.

I used to walk from Ember Lane to the middle of Home Park and back because that year, of all years, I was doing my year of hard labour in Colditz, the name that we gave to the Stud nursery. I was still in the middle of my seven-year apprenticeship and the system was that every six months or a year you were moved to a different part of the grounds for training plus one day a week in college and various institutions, such as Kew, Wisley, Merrist Wood, Malling Research Centre and Waterperry in Oxford, to learn various techniques of the trade.

The training I treasured most, and the hardest to endure, was the stint in Colditz. It was an old walled garden attached to Stud House and was once a favourite residence of King George 1V. After the war, Hampton Court took over this neglected garden and, with the help of German prisoners of war, cleaned it up and made a tree and shrub nursery under the supervision of an old gardener and his wife. Like all characters he had a nickname. He was a short little man with beady, bright blue eyes and a mouthful of black teeth, which could be seen at the odd times he laughed, usually at someone's misfortune. He always said that he wasn't in the room when God gave out the good looks, so he was known as 'Mr. Quilp' from *The Old Curiosity Shop* by Charles Dickens on account of the way he ran the nursery. The discipline was so severe and the work so hard that you either came to Colditz to learn, as I did, or you were forced to resign or get the sack.

At my first showing round, I was amazed at everything. It was immaculate, with straight lines of every sort of plant and tree, some rarely seen, spotless greenhouses, naked paths and fan-trained fruit trees with branches measured to six inches apart. Tools were washed and oiled every night, paths of sieved clinker were raked every Friday and everything was faultless. I was willing to learn, and it instilled in me how to be a perfectionist for life.

The snow came and every day it got colder and colder, yet we still worked out in it, digging, as he would have all the vacant ground covered in leaves so that it would not freeze and would keep our feet dry. The leaves were trenched in to keep the ground moist in winter, something I still do today. With the number of plots I have, there's no time to water plants more than the once they get when I settle them in. After that, it's up to them! Every day we would get our orders and watch as the snow got thicker and thicker on the branches of the giant cedars in Stud House. With three feet of snow on them the weight must have been enormous, and they just seemed to groan in the ice-cold wind. After a while work was getting scarce. All the pots were clean, the leaf and manure heaps turned to generate heat (and keep us warm), the logs cut, the labels cleaned and all the winter jobs completed – and still it snowed. The road to Stud House was cleared every day but the snow was so deep that even the sheep and deer in the park had to be dug out and we all used to help the shepherd whose dog would find them completely covered in snow. After eight hours' hard labour it was then the long walk back to Esher.

> "A short little man with beady, bright blue eyes and a mouthful of black teeth."

Looking back, I can't thank that old gardener enough for his teaching. He and I got on so well, despite his discipline and hard ways, and it set me up with high standards and respect. The country kept going until the thaw in March and I survived my year at the nursery. After my apprenticeship finished, I went back to learn more for another year which had never been done before. The old chap retired to a cottage in Devon in the 'Camellia county' that he had always loved but, sadly, died a year later. However, he left a wonderful legacy for me in his understanding of plants, how to produce and grow them well and how to create and manage the earth: not taking without putting back, and a bit like life really, the way you are towards your fellow men.

Camellias

BEFORE CHRISTMAS I AM AMAZED AT THE FLOOD OF CAMELLIAS IN THE garden centres. Ideal gifts at reasonable prices. When I started my career, they were a plant only for the rich as they were tender and had to be kept under glass in the winter.

My first encounter with a camellia was in the orchard at the Palace. This was a very private place where the ladies in the Grace and Favour apartments cultivated their own plants and flowers. In a corner I noticed a tall, wooden contraption covered in straw and was told by the old gardener that it was Mrs. Bruce's camellia, brought down by her from Scotland. "Blodwen looks after it," he said. I assumed that this was Mrs Bruce's Welsh companion but, oh, no, it was the nickname for the Palace dustman. He was a round little man in a boiler suit, black beret and pebble glasses and possessed only two teeth. He was often seen carrying a large bucket of tea leaves which were for feeding the camellia! As a matter of interest, the tea plant is called *Camellia sinensis* so that did make sense. Apparently, he collected tea leaves from all the residents as well as his main duty which was to collect the ash from the fires: this was, of course, long before central heating and the heat all came from coal and log fires. Every Friday he would burn the rubbish in an old incinerator. The smoke was awful and blew over the wall and on to the greenhouses so once we got a ladder and a hosepipe to put out his fire. It was quite amusing to see this little figure in wet overalls and splattered glasses shouting abuse at us in Welsh!

Our superintendent was also besotted by camellias and had, on leaving his earlier employment at a large country estate, purchased their camellia collection and brought it to the Palace. Raised beds were constructed and filled with peaty loam, the edges being retained by blocks of heather, laid so that the heather grew into the beds. The camellias were in these beds along and behind the Maze, being a unique collection from Nymans Garden in Sussex. Some of my favourites were 'Salutation', 'Inspiration', 'Donation' and many others.

In the very hard winter of 1963, a pipe burst in a nearby building and water poured out onto the camellia bed and particularly onto a fine specimen of 'Donation'. It was Christmas and no plumber would come out to repair the pipe, so the water kept on flowing. As it flowed, it froze, and soon the plant was encased in a solid block of ice. In the new year the Royal Horticultural Society came to photograph for their magazine, and we all wondered if it would survive. The thaw came in March and, lo and behold, it emerged unscathed and was covered in blooms by Easter. So it proved to be a very hardy variety and justly deserves its 'Award of Merit' certificate.

It's a what?

WATCHING ONE OF THE BETTER GARDENING PROGRAMMES ABOUT allotments on a huge site in Birmingham and in particular, a plot where a self-sown cannabis plant had popped up, it reminded me of my days as a trainee gardener at the Stud House. Locally known as Colditz owing to the way it was run by a very strict military-type gardener and his wife, you went there either for training, as we did, or were sent there for disciplining as the last stop before the sack.

At the Stud House, I worked with a colleague of mine called Tony who by the way, had a great interest in the drug and poison potential of plants. One day he tried out an arum lily and cheese sandwich on me and I ended up in the Intensive Care Unit for three days! He later went on to take charge of the Botanical Gardens of Bermuda, but we still meet up.

One day we were trenching when I decided to clean out my pockets that contained some old birdseed and broken biscuits which I used to feed the birds. It's a life-long habit as I have kept birds all my life – the feathered ones I mean, having never married myself! A couple of weeks later, up came this seedling that grew at an alarming rate, with beautiful pinnate leaves. It was soon noticed by the old head gardener who knew all the plants but, obviously, not cannabis. Only my mate Tony and I knew what it was and so we kept it as our little secret. As it grew, it was tended, fed, tied up, and shown to everyone of importance who visited the Palace. This was now taken to be a wonderful acer of such quick growth, (which wasn't common in acers) until, one day, the head of the Royal Parks came on his annual inspection. He was a major who had served in the Far East and, of course, he was shown the wonderful new shrub, at which point his eyes nearly popped out. "It's cannabis, not an acer!" he screamed. "Pull it up now and destroy it." This was the worst thing that could have happened: growing drugs in a park of a royal residence! The embarrassment on the 'high-ups' faces was very great.

I still always carry birdseed and broken biscuits to feed any little birds who might be hungry. The crumbed biscuits also serve another purpose. When I am asked for change by an ill-mannered shop assistant who doesn't say 'please', I gladly give them change covered in biscuit crumbs, much to their annoyance. They have to wipe it clean before putting it in the till. 'Please' is such a little word, rarely used today but it means a lot. Manners cost nothing.

Reunion walk

EVERY SO OFTEN, WHAT'S LEFT OF THE OLD STAFF FROM MY DAY HAVE A reunion at the Palace when we walk round the park and gardens and see what has disappeared in the name of 'conservation'.

We arrived at our meeting place and gazed up at the giant poplar trees which I remember holding as little sticks in my hand. It was Maundy Thursday and one of those jobs that 'won't take long to pop in'. They were a special variety, a gift from Kew.

When you climbed a ladder at the palace you got an assistant, a young lad or an apprentice to train. This was my first encounter with Little Ted, who would go on to share in a great many adventures, some of which I have talked about already. At this time, he had just joined the staff and was a short little chap dressed in black with a cap that never came off, pebble glasses and ill-fitting dentures which, no matter in what company, he would take out for a clean with a matchstick and a quick rinse in a pond or waterway. We all said that the cartoonist Giles must have used him as a model! To cap it all, he had been a gravedigger all his life, so every tree was planted six feet deep and thrived. The poplars were to be planted on the site of the now demolished American camp so every time we dug a hole, we hit rubble or concrete so it was a week or so before all the six foot holes were excavated and the 'sticks' planted and watered and eventually grew to the lovely specimens that are now enjoyed by a new generation.

As we walked up towards Teddington, enjoying the deer rutting, we were saddened at the sad state of Wren's chestnut avenue. Wren said that one day the avenue would look like a 'million chandeliers' but for how much longer we wondered?

We were also involved in the restoration of the Maze, renewing it with yews instead of the clipped mixture of rough hedging that it was when I first joined. Every year large sections were pulled out and replaced with six-foot high, two-foot wide, clipped yews. Each had been root-pruned some two or three years previously and then left to develop a fibrous root system so that when planted out with tender loving care and water, it grew away. Preparation is the guarantee of success. We all know what happens to seed that falls on stony ground!

Every year I make a point of planting at least one tree somewhere for a future generation to enjoy. This year it will be a yew, the symbol of immortality and everlasting life.

A goodly heritage*

LOOKING BACK ON LIFE IT HAS ALWAYS AMAZED ME THAT GOOD ALWAYS seems to come out of bad in some way or another. Looking at the lovely uniformity of the limes on the east front of Hampton Court Palace the other day I remembered the opposition from all sides when the then Superintendent, Mr Fisher, wanted to remove the old trees that Charles II had planted. They had become dangerous and were always falling down crushing their younger replacements. Then came the great hurricane and they were all down in one night and a new lot of the same size replaced them not long after. Looking at them now, all so perfect, just shows how great God is and how good has come out of bad.

Another of Mr Fisher's projects was planned for the wilderness area of the gardens. He had always wanted to create a vista through the chestnut avenue in Bushy Park through Lion Gate and expose the Great Hall as the huge elm trees obscured this. Lo and behold, the county was indeed ravaged by Dutch elm disease so those big elms had to be cleared, and the vista was created. One tree was left, a quite mature Amelanchier from Canada planted by the widow of Field Marshall Birdwood who had been 'grace and favour' residents. Every year, on the anniversary of his death, she would be brought to the park to see it. Because of the plan for the vista, it was proposed to try and move it about thirty feet away without her knowing and, as she always came in September, Ted and I started our biggest conquest. We took months preparing the tree and the hole and finally it was dragged out by two tractors and much manpower, placed in the giant hole, fed, watered and staked.

---

* Psalm 16 v6 from the King James Bible: 'The lines are fallen unto me in pleasant places; yea I have a goodly heritage'

Everyone involved kept their fingers crossed (and, I might say, their mouths shut!) and when, in the spring it burst into growth we all breathed a sigh of relief. His widow, well into her nineties, never noticed that it had been moved but, strange to say, that tree never grew any bigger but only thicker with age and is still there, by the way!

Mr Fisher's other great accomplishment was to create, from a rubbish dump, the Woodland Garden in Bushy Park with its wildlife lakes, one of which is named after him. Ted and I planted lots of trees in there years ago and I like to go back on quiet days with my memories and look at what we did and give thanks to God for that bit of creation we left for other generations to enjoy.

The secret to a long life?

THE WEATHER FORECAST FOR THIS YEAR, WHICH WAS ALL GLOOM AND doom, has resulted in the hottest summer ever! Sometimes I think that the weather men couldn't run a bath let alone a meteorological office. This year has been wonderful in the garden, especially for fruit and, of course, weeds, slugs and blights. Strange weather patterns were with us in the seventeenth century and show up in the growth rings on ancient trees.

May and June used to be the busiest months at the Palace, when the beds were changed to summer planting. All the ground was hand dug a foot deep, and days were long: seven in the morning till eight at night. The ground would be rock hard, and the clods of earth had to be broken down with the back of a spade. In the evenings the beds would be thoroughly watered ready to plant the next morning. The heat was often unbearable, with 'flaming June' days, which were very hard to endure, but everyone did. We were a tougher race then and these days I suppose regulations wouldn't allow us to work so many long hours.

Now I'm ready for the next sunny day when I shall tackle the seedling weeds. This is not like the old days at Hampton Court when certain days meant certain jobs were started. For example, the Great Vine would be pruned two weeks before Christmas and then the vents were left open to let in frosty cold air to make sure it went dormant and rested before being warmed up again in February. Then there was a certain day when the tulip beds were cleared. Ladies Day at Ascot was the start of the hedge cutting, including the Maze, just when the children were on holiday and would delight in climbing through the hedges to push you off the ladders for fun. We had ways of getting our own back and now there is an iron spiked fence through the hedge!

This is where I introduce Henry. Like other staff he had a nickname, 'Mantis'. Henry was quite a character. A tall, thin man of six foot seven who always wore blue overalls and an old brown cap and did everything in slow motion: all the characteristics of a praying mantis. Every single day, winter or summer, Henry had a ploughman's lunch with fruits and vegetables he had grown on one of his allotments. His official job was to drive a huge old grey Massey Ferguson tractor. On Fridays he always rolled the Broad Walk with an aged giant steamroller which took all day and part of Saturday. He never drove anywhere at more than fifteen miles an hour and you can imagine the holdups in the parks, where he drove in the middle of the road making sure that everyone else kept to the speed limit. Certainly, there was no need for speed traps when he was on the road. I used to help Henry round up the herds of cattle he looked after, sometimes riding bikes across the park on a bright, frosty morning, though I wanted to go a bit faster than he did, just to keep warm.

> "Ladies Day at Ascot was the start of the hedge cutting,"

The digging of the beds on the East Front was a shattering experience for us, all in very high temperatures in blazing sun. In the evening and night, Henry would water them with the giant hose pipes ready for planting the next day. He loved this job as it was overtime for him and, as we all understood, he was under "petticoat rule" at home. He loved a drink so, at night, he drank and watered. We often found him asleep the next morning under one of the giant yew trees and, yes, with the hose still running! Fortunately, we were not on a meter as the water supply came from the Longford River which still runs from a spring under the airport miles away. One water system was installed in Wolsey's time and the other ran from Coombe Hill under the Thames. Very clever people in the 15th century!

Of course, Henry's watering methods were slow but they were thorough, in spite of his evening refreshments. He could calculate how much to soak a bed so that it would be just right to plant the next morning without it being too 'mucky'. He always got the job done. Henry, like the tortoise, reached a great age, a hundred and one. There must be something to be said for a slower pace of life and the secret to a long life.

I guess if we have just one night's frost this winter, the so-called experts will be predicting another Ice Age for us, who knows?

Sparky meets his Waterloo

THERE IS A BRIDLE PATH RUNNING IN FRONT OF THE HOUSE THROUGH THE woods and, over the years, I have got to know all the horses and dogs by name, except for the one or two who don't want to speak to a grubby gnome! The other day I decided to get the mower out and start it up after the winter rest when along came a young lady on a rather highly strung hunter. As she approached our gates the piston came out, making a loud bang and frightening her horse and me. After getting it under control she gave me a lot of verbal abuse, (which I won't repeat) to which I calmly replied, "Well, the Duke of Wellington didn't have that trouble on his horse," to which she replied, "this is Claygate Woods not (bleep) Waterloo."

The incident reminded me of my old days at the Palace. When the administration changed, one of the top bureaucrats decided that all creatures employed in the parks should report once a week to the office! That included the shepherds' and gamekeepers' dogs, the hawk kept for pigeon control on the Palace and the park keeper's old horse, Sparky. Now Sparky had two speeds, first gear and stop, generally for a pat or a tit-bit. You knew if he was crossing the road from Bushy Park into the gardens by the traffic jams over the bridge and down to Kingston, and he didn't like noises or cars.

One day the old park keeper who rode him was too ill and a new, somewhat arrogant, young keeper was sent down from Hyde Park armed with crop and spurs to make Sparky go faster and be more obedient. His attitude upset a number of people especially my little mate Ted, of whom I've written before. One day the young keeper rode him using his crop and spurs quite a lot on the old horse and I could tell from looking at Ted's beady eyes behind his pebble glasses that something was on his mind.

A couple of days later we knew, from seeing the stationary traffic, that

Sparky was on his way and suddenly Ted left us. Now in the wilderness at the back of the cafeteria was a fenced off area where the dustbins were kept and you'll remember that Sparky didn't like sudden, loud noises. As the horse approached the fence a loud clash of bin lids went off, and so did Sparky, with the young keeper on top of him. He eventually managed to stop him and got off, shaken, and then started to hit the old horse. However, some members of the public spotted this and reported the incident, and he was promptly sent back to Hyde Park. Little Ted was never found out and after work I was allowed to take Sparky out and ride him around Bushy Park in the evenings until his master recovered.

Sparky died peacefully in his paddock and was buried in the park near the Woodland Garden by the few of us who were special to him. I sometimes stand on the spot and remember the fun we had with two-speed Sparky, even though it wasn't Waterloo.

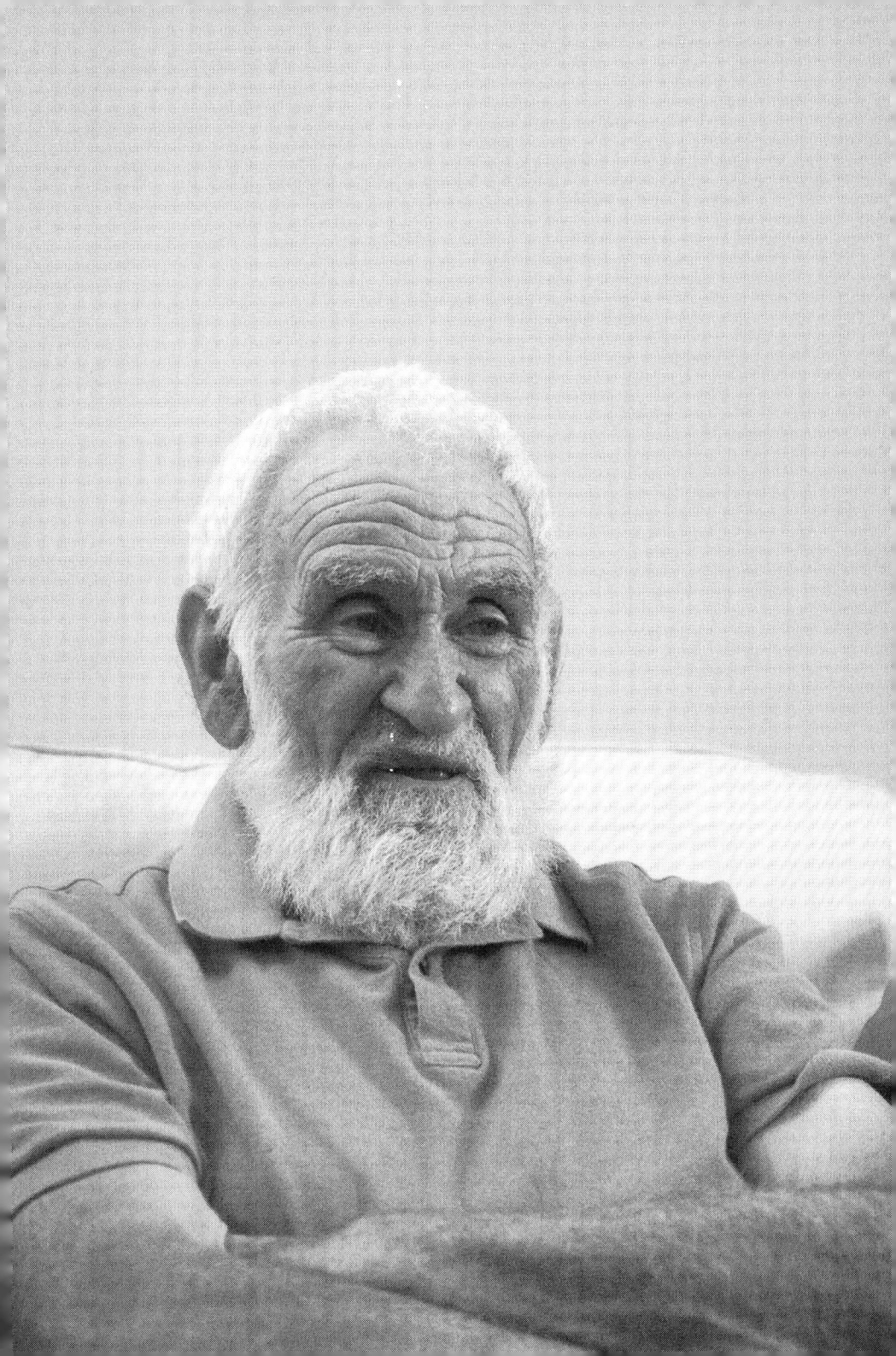

Acknowledgements

I thank first those who have shaped this book. To Gerald Smith, without whose intriguing life and an incredible ability to recount it so vividly, I could not have put this book together. The significance of the people within Gerald's stories cannot be underestimated and I thank them (mostly posthumously) for their contributions. Instrumental in the initial process of transferring Gerald's original notes into a series of pamphlets some years ago, my heartfelt thanks go to Cloe Dwelly. Having recently recorded additional stories with Gerald to include here, it has been a pleasure to build on Cloe's foresight. For so readily assisting me in locating sources of local historical images and maps I am indebted to Pam Tiller, who has given me private access to the excellent archive collection of All Saints Weston Green.

For help in the journey to publication I have first to thank my good friend Alison Cruthers for asking me more than once to embark on this project. As Churchwarden at All Saints, she has been a superb and highly efficient collaborator enabling meetings, conversations and decisions allowing us to complete publication in a very short time! To Revd. Richard Rugg, I am so very grateful to you and the whole church family for your immediate willingness to welcome me into your lives, often with rather too many questions.

Without the superb professionalism and expert guidance of my long-standing friend and colleague, Annette Peppis this book could not have progressed beyond my compilation and edit. I have relied heavily upon Annette's step by step guidance and project management and have thoroughly enjoyed every part of the process.

I am very grateful for permission to use the photographs on pp2, 10, 60, 105 and the back cover which are by Glyn Jones. The portrait of Gerald on the front cover (which was painted as a gift by his friend John White) was also photographed by Glyn.

Lastly, my thanks and appreciation are due to the friends of mine who live in our local area and who, it turns out, also know Gerald in one way or another and are now eager to see the finished product.

Communities are the essence of neighbourhoods and localities, and if this little volume helps to further connect ours, then Gerald's 'Slice of Life' will have been even more worthwhile.

Julia Jones
Compiler and editor

Credits

Photos by Glyn Jones on pp2, 10, 60, 105 and back cover (portrait).
Cover background photo by A. Mahmood on Unsplash.
Illustrations on pp36, 40, 44, 52, 64, 74, 80, 86, 102, by Oleksandra Klestova/Shutterstock
Digital manipulation on cover by Lewis Golland